# Marquetry & Inlay

## 18 Decorative Projects

Alan & Gill Bridgewater

TAB BOOKS

Blue Ridge Summit, PA

FIRST EDITION
SECOND PRINTING

© 1991 by **TAB Books**.
TAB Books is a division of McGraw-Hill, Inc.

**Library of Congress Cataloging-in-Publication Data**

Bridgewater, Alan.
   Marquetry and inlay : 18 decorative projects / by Alan and Gill
Bridgewater.
     p.    cm.
   Includes bibliographical references and index.
   ISBN 0-8306-8426-3    ISBN 0-8306-3426-6 (pbk.)
   1. Marquetry.  I. Bridgewater, Gill.  II. Title.
TT192.B75  1991
745.51—dc20
                                      90-48857
                                      CIP

TAB Books offers software for sale. For information and a catalog, please contact
TAB Software Department, Blue Ridge Summit, PA 17294-0850.

Acquisitions Editor: Kimberly Tabor
Book Editor: April D. Nolan
Production: Katherine G. Brown
Book Design: Jaclyn J. Boone

# Contents

# Acknowledgments

We would like to thank our two sons, Glyn and Julian, for their help making the various marquetry and inlay items. What a time we had!

We would also like to thank Caroline White and family—of Art Veneers Co. Ltd. of Mildenhall, Suffolk, England—for their help with materials, literature, kits, advice, and sponsorship.

# Introduction

**M**arquetry and inlay were inspired by the ancient craft of *intarsia*—the making of decorative and pictorial mosaics by the inlaying of precious and exotic materials into or onto a groundwork of solid wood.

Three thousand or so years ago, the Egyptians decorated much of their woodwork with inlay. In fact, in the tomb of the Pharaoh King Tutankhamon, the throne, chest, coffers, and nearly all the furniture are literally covered with inlay (FIG. I-1). Precious stones, miniature glazed tiles, and little brickets of wood, gold and ivory wonderfully embellished items of special prestigious and ceremonial importance.

In the Orient—in Persia, India, China and Japan—inlay workers created all sorts of decorative delights, from complex wood parquetry designs set into floors to wood mosaics on walls and furniture, to small inlay picture designs on boxes, caskets, tombs, reliquaries and ceremonial regalia. All uniquely beautiful, and all fabulously expensive in terms of time, labor and cost of materials.

Through the centuries, in ancient Egypt, Imperial Rome, Persia, eighth-century Japan, and sixteenth-century Italy and Germany, rich patrons employed inlay craftsmen to create beautiful works of art (FIG. I-2). The process was both expensive and painstaking because, traditionally, the craft involved many long steps: importing rare and exotic hardwoods; slowly carving, lowering, and trenching a groundwork; sawing and slicing the small amount of difficult-to-cut, expensive hardwood into $1/4-1/2$-inch-thick tiles; fitting and setting the mosaic tiles into a bed of glue or mastic, one piece at a time; and then finally scraping, rubbing down, waxing, and burnishing the inlay surface.

And so it might have continued, had not an anonymous German clockmaker invented the jigsaw blade near the end of the sixteenth century. The blade made possible new mass-production methods. No longer was the craft slow and prohibitively expensive, nor was it greedily gobbling up vast amounts of rare exotic woods. With the revolutionary fast-moving, frame-held saw blade, it was possible to double, triple and even quadruple production simply by repeatedly cutting the expensive slab woods into thinner and thinner sheets. Better still, it was also possible to sandwich stacks of veneers together and cut six or so designs all at once.

**I-I** Detail from the back of Tutankhamon's ceremonial chair—intricately inlaid with precious stones, glazed tiles and wood, all set in sheet gold—(Egypt 1350 BC).

As they say, the rest is all history. From the seventeenth century (FIG. I-3) right through to the end of the nineteenth century, tools improved, and techniques became increasingly swifter and more refined. By the end of the nineteenth century, thin inlay veneer, or *marquetry* as it had now come to be called, was an extremely popular and accessible form of furniture decoration (FIGS. I-4 and I-5). The early twentieth century heralded a revival of interest in special high-quality, exotic wood inlays and marquetries, with designers, hobbyists and artists creating pieces considered works of art in their own right (FIG. I-6).

I sometimes look at my collection of veneers and miserly marvel at the colors, the uniquely beautiful grain patterns, and the rich aromas. I get a great deal of pleasure from handling the precious woods and reading off the wonderfully evocative names and descriptions: Rich, brown ebony from the Celebes Islands, blood-red padouk from the Andaman Islands, red pau rosa from West Africa, primavera from Central America, satinwood, teak, tola and zebrano—all pure poetry. Each name evokes storybook pictures of teak forests, Burmese elephants hauling trees, huge river rafts of logs, and jungle saw mills.

**I-2**  Detail from a Nonesuch chest with holly and bog oak inlay, parquetry, and marquetry. (Late sixteenth century.)

**I-3**  Detail from an English marquetry box, about 1670. Worked with sand scorched and toned walnut veneers on a dark ground. Note the delicate realism of the bird and the foliage.

**I-4** Detail from an English Tunbridgeware games board, about 1830. The Tunbridgeware technique is a delicate form of a sliced-stick miniature-mosaic parquetry and marquetry.

**I-5** Cube parquetry box, thought to have been made in Tunbridge Wells, England, at the beginning of the nineteenth century.

**I-6** Detail from a 1920s standing cabinet. A *bal masque* lady in fancy dress, worked in at least ten different veneers.

I sometimes run my fingertips across one of my marquetries and marvel at its soft, silky textures and the wonderful, subtle shine of the figure and the rays—so beautiful! To look at the delicate patterns and the crisply curved forms and to remember the hours spent cutting, scoring, trimming, fitting, gluing, sanding and polishing—these are all part and parcel of marquetry and inlay. These are all uniquely uplifting and stimulating craft experiences that should not be missed.

With such items to make and decorate as cube parquetry mats, floral marquetry pictures, a games board, an Egyptian inlay valet figure, an art deco mirror frame, and a Nonesuch inlay, this book will allow you to share in all the hands-on-tool pleasures of marquetry and inlay.

No problem if you are a beginner. In the glossary section at the beginning of the book, we describe in detail the various tools, techniques, materials, and terms. In addition, with the 18 step-by-step projects, we set out to give you all the answers. With short introductions, project pictures, gridded and scaled working drawings, and complete illustrations throughout, we guide you gently through all the making stages—drawing up the design, transferring the imagery, making first cuts, fitting, fixing, gluing, finishing, and so on.

There are some tools/materials you will need for every project in this book. They are:

- a plastic cutting mat.
- a scalpel and a pack of spare blades.
- a roll of low-tack masking tape.
- a cork sanding block.
- a pack of graded glass/garnet papers.
- an assortment of pencils, to include a 2B and a 3H.
- a compass.
- a steel cutting ruler.

At the end of the book, there is a pattern and motif directory. If you are looking for motif or pattern inspiration—again, no problem. The series of scale-gridded designs will help you on your way. Don't get me wrong—we do aim to guide you every step of the way, but this isn't one of those books where the projects are so boringly easy that they aren't worth doing anyway. Believe you me, each project will, in some way or other, present you with a good, solid, worthwhile challenge.

As you work through the various projects, you will see that we have suggested all manner of exciting traditional and nontraditional variations and modifications. This is not to say that you need to make each marquetry or inlay in a completely different way. Rather, you should consider all the tool-and-technique implications of the various projects, and go for the approach that best suits you.

The book's 200 or so drawings leave no stone unturned, and each project relates to or is inspired by a specific marquetry or inlay tradition or technique. We hope the beginner will increase his or her knowledge, expertise, and confidence, and along the way create marquetry and inlay articles that are uniquely beautiful.

# Glossary

**Ash** Europe/USA   A cream-colored veneer with a dark, wavy grain. Width from 8–15 inches.

**Aspen** (Europe)   A cream to yellow veneer, good for sky effects; sometimes has a beautiful, streaky-pink grain. Width 8–14 inches.

**Ayan** (West Africa)   A yellow to brown veneer, a bit like Satinwood. Width 8–14 inches.

**Banding**   Long strips of geometrically patterned inlay; ready-to-use strips that come in a wide variety of styles, designs and patterns.

**Baseboard**   The ground, base, or panel on or in which the marquetry or inlay is set. If you have a choice, best go for top-quality, white-faced multicore plywood—in which case the rule of thumb is: the larger the panel, the thicker the ply (FIG. G-1).

**Beech** (Europe/USA)   A cream-white veneer with a delicately flecked figure. Width 8–10 inches.

**Bench Hook**   A simple, easy-to-make hooked form used for steadying and supporting the workpiece when sawing. It is made up from a base, a front edge piece, and a rest (FIG. G-2).

**Birch** (Canada)   A creamy brown veneer with a wavy water-marked figure. Width 8–14 inches.

**Birdsmouth Board**   Sometimes called a V-board, a small table with a V-end profile; used in conjunction with a coping, fret, or piecing saw. In use, the board is clamped to a table so that the V end projects over the edge.

**Blemishes**   In the context of this book, a blemish is anything that detracts from the quality of the workpiece. Of course, in terms of veneer grain, color, and figure, one man's blemish might be another man's perfect design feature. Choose your veneers with care.

**Blister**   A pocket of air between the marquetry assembly and the base board; such a fault needs to be sorted out before you start rubbing down and polishing. Cut into the blister with the point of the scalpel, then squeeze a small amount of white PVA glue into the cavity and reclamp.

**Boulle**   Boulle work, sometimes called *boule* or *buhl*, is brilliantly colored and variously composed of wood, brass, tortoiseshell and ivory. The key to boulle designs is their identical but contrasting counterchange effect (FIG. G-3).

**G-I** Always make sure the baseboard is clean, stable, and smooth. To this end, use a scraper to take the wood to a level finish.

**G-2** When using a bench hook, be sure the wood to be cut is butted hard up against the rest.

**G-3** The boulle technique involves sawing and working a multi-material "sandwich" and swapping over the cutouts to create identical but contrasting counterchange designs.

**Boxwood** (Europe and S. America)   A close-grained cream veneer; easy to cut and work; good for thin inlay lines and delicate motifs. Width 4–8 inches.

**Brushes**   Marquetry and inlay workers need a good selection of brushes for touching up details, gluing, varnishing, and so on. Buy the most expensive, and keep them clean and dry.

**Burbinga** (West Africa)   A reddish-brown veneer with dark red stripes. Width 8–14 inches.

**Callipers**   A two-legged drawing/measuring instrument; can be used for stepping off measurements, for scribing circles, for drawing out a motif, and for measuring inside and outside diameters. All marquetry and inlay workers need a pair of callipers.

**Carbon Paper**   Black carbon paper is used in conjunction with a hard pencil or a ballpoint pen for press transferring traced designs through to veneers. Avoid permanent blue-dye carbon paper.

**Caul Veneering**   In the context of this book, an arrangement of boards, plastic sheet, newspaper, battens and clamps, as might be used for pressing and clamping veneers and marquetry assemblies. Traditionally, veneering cauls are shaped to fit specific furniture designs and profiles.

**Cedar of Lebanon** (Lebanon)   A rich biscuit-colored veneer with a delicate strip and a pleasant aroma. Width 8−14 inches.

**Cherry** (Europe and USA)   A reddish veneer. Width 8−10 inches.

**Chestnut** (Europe)   Several types—varies from white through to light brown. Horse Chestnut is often used for white banding strips. Width 6−12 inches.

**Clamps (Cramps, Holdfasts)**   Screw devices used for holding veneer and marquetry assemblies while they are being glued down onto the base or ground wood. They are also called G-clamps, C-clamps, strap clamps and so on. In use, the workpiece is sandwiched between plastic sheet, boards, and battens and the clamps are tightened up (FIG. G-4).

**Compasses**   A two-legged instrument used for drawing circles and arcs. Best to get a long-legged, multipurpose, screw-operated type.

**Compensating Veneer**   A large sheet of veneer, as might be glued on the back of a marquetry composition. If the marquetry is mounted on a thin ground, say a sheet

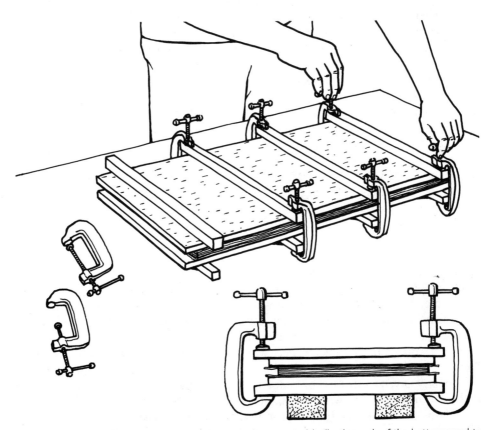

**G-4**  When clamping several layers, aim for an even pressure. Ideally, the ends of the battens need to be slightly rounded or tapered so that as you tighten the clamps, the pressure will begin at the center and force the surplus glue out toward the edges.

of plywood, then it requires a compensating veneer to keep the plywood sheet structurally stable and balanced. Note: Although it is recommended practice to veneer both sides of a sheet of plywood, if you are only working a small project, leave out the backing veneer.

**Contact Adhesive (impact adhesive)** A low-stress adhesive. In use, it is smeared thinly over both surfaces. After 15–20 minutes, the two surfaces are brought together. There are now easy-to-use, water-based varieties.

**Coping Saw** A fine-bladed frame saw used for fretting out thin-section ground wood and thick veneers. A good general-purpose saw for making up groundworks, boxes, frames and so on. The blade can be quickly removed and refitted, so this is the perfect saw for ground work and for working tight corners and curves. Note: Coping saw blades have pins at both ends, so they can only be used for edge cuts and large holes.

**Cork Block** A block used to support glass/garnet paper; used to rub down large flat surfaces.

**Counterchanging** The technique of sandwiching veneers, cutting through the layers, and then changing the cutouts around so as to create a color texture counterchange. See also **Boulle**.

**Craft Knife** A general-purpose knife used for cutting paper, card, thick veneers, sheet wood and string. Best to have one with a short, securely-fixed, easy-to-change blade.

**Crossbanding** A veneer edge strip or border where the grain runs at right angles to the edge of the object being covered.

**Cutting board/mat** A work surface used when knife-cutting veneers. Although you can use just about any clean, flat surface, it is best to use a semi-hard, rubber-like plastic mat. Such a surface allows the knife to bite, but leaves the surface of the board unmarked.

**Designing** Achieving forms, details, and motifs by visiting museums, looking around art galleries, making drawings and keeping a sketch book. We draw much of our inspiration from traditional works.

**Dents** A shallow dent can be remedied by dropping a small amount of water into the dent, covering it with a sheet of brown paper, and heating it with an electric iron. The wet, hot wood fibers swell and rise to fill the dent.

**Drafting Paper** *See* tracing paper.

**Drilling Holes** Best to work with an easy-to-use, silent-running, hand-operated drill. In use, support the work with a waster, check the angle of the drill with a set square, and secure the wood with a clamp. Hold and steady the drill with one hand, and set it in motion with the other.

**Elm** (England) A brown-green veneer with a mild, stripy figure. Width 8–12 inches.

**Exotic** In the context of this book, an exotic veneer is one that originates in another country; a veneer that has beautiful, rare or attractive qualities.

**Felt-tip Pens** Ordinary water- or spirit-based felt-nibbed pens. Details, edges and part-motifs can be colored with felt tips and then varnished.

**Figure** The pattern of the grain as seen on the surface of a veneer. Figure designs and shapes relate to the frequency of growth rings, to color, to tree types, to how the tree is cut, and so on. Characteristic figure patterns have such names as "pencil striped," "quilted," "fiddle back," and "beeswing."

**Filler** Used to fill breaks, cavities and scratches. You can use two-tube resin fillers for large cracks, woodstopping pastes for small splits and holes, colored wax sticks for color-matching repairs on furniture, and paste grain fillers on coarse veneers, where the surface needs to be worked up to a high finish. Note: If you save sawdust in labelled bottles, it can be mixed with white PVA adhesive and used as the perfect-match filler.

**Finishing** The process of filling, sanding, rubbing down, staining, varnishing, waxing, framing, mounting and otherwise bringing the work to a satisfactory structural, textural, and visual conclusion.

**Fit-and-Fix** The act of putting together—fitting, fixing, gluing, pinning, nailing, screwing, and sticking with tape.

**Fretsaw** Belongs to the same family as piercing and coping saws. They have "G" frames and flexible, removable blades; a good saw for cutting holes and curves in thin section plywood and for cutting veneers. In use, the frame is guided and steadied with one hand, while the handle is pushed and maneuvered with the other. *See also* coping saw and piercing saw.

**G-clamps or C-clamps** *See* clamps.

**Gluefilm (thermoplastic gluefilm)** A paper-backed roll of thermoplastic adhesive. Such a glue is easy to use because you don't need a press and it allows you to rework a bubbled or blistered area (FIG. G-5).

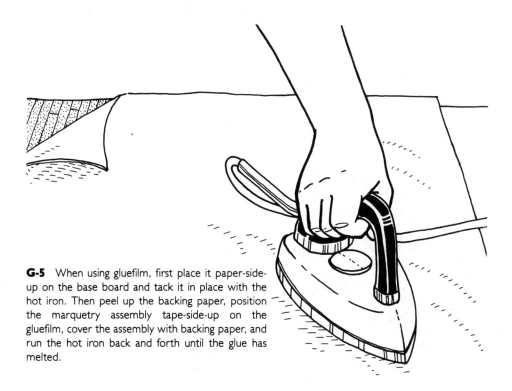

**G-5** When using gluefilm, first place it paper-side-up on the base board and tack it in place with the hot iron. Then peel up the backing paper, position the marquetry assembly tape-side-up on the gluefilm, cover the assembly with backing paper, and run the hot iron back and forth until the glue has melted.

**Gridded Working Drawing**   In the context of this book, a gridded working drawing is a drawing or illustration that has been drawn on a scaled grid. If you want to change the scale, all you do is draw up a larger grid, and transfer the image one square at a time.

**Groundwork**   *See* base board.

**Hammers**   In the context of this book, use either a 4-ounce ball-peen or a cross-peen hammer, and hold it toward the end of the handle.

**Hand Drill**   *See* drilling.

**Harewood**   Veneers produced by chemically treating certain other woods to create various silver green/gray/blue veneers.

**Holly** (USA)   A white/cream colored, close-grained, easy-to-work veneer; turns light brown with age. Width 5−8 inches.

**Inlay**   The craft of setting one wood within another (FIG. G-6).

**Inspirational Designs**   In the context of this book, inspirational designs refer to marquetries and inlays that you have seen in museums and shops, manufacturers literature, old book, our designs, and so on.

**G-6**   Inlay requires that the base wood be lowered, trenched, grooved, or otherwise cut away, and the inlay wood set in the lowered area so that it is flush with the surface.

**Impact Adhesive**  *See* contact adhesive.

**Iroko** (West Africa)  A deep yellow/brown, oily veneer with an interesting mottle. Width 8−12 inches.

**Jig**  In the context of this book, a jig is a simple device used for multiple-cutting veneers. (FIG. G-7).

**Kingwood** (Brazil)  A deep rich brown veneer with black shading. Width 3−6 inches.

**Lacewood** (England)  A pinkish, beautifully figured veneer with characteristic lacey rays. Width 6−10 inches.

**Jewelers Saw**  *See* piercing saw.

**Lime** (Europe)  A creamy, white/yellow veneer with a smooth, easy-to-work grain. Width 4−12 inches.

**Low-tack Tape**  Just about any sticky-contact masking or clear plastic tape that you might use to hold marquetry assemblies prior to gluing. We use ordinary masking tape (FIG. G-8).

**Maple** (Canada)  A creamy-white, easy-to-work veneer. Width 6−18 inches.

**Master Design**  The final measured working drawing; the drawing from which all the details are taken.

**Matching**  The process of joining sheets of veneer together so as to make a larger patterned sheet. As consecutive veneer leaves are cut from the tree, they are tied in

**G-7**  Using a jig. In this instance, a batten stop and a 1-inch-wide metal straightedge are used to cut and work a number of identical 1-inch-wide strips of veneer.

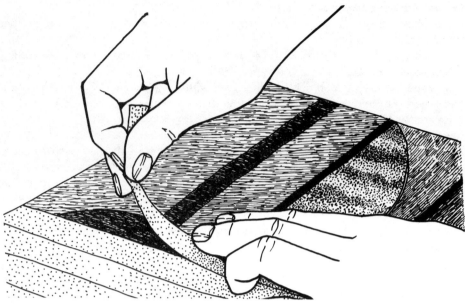

**G-8**  You can use ordinary masking tape to hold marquetry assemblies together prior to gluing.

bundles of 24, 28 and 32. These veneer leaves can be variously cut, placed and arranged to create traditional designs and patterns.

**Modifying**   The process of changing and generally redesigning all or part of the project to suit your own needs.

**Muffled Vice**   If a delicate, partially made workpiece needs to be held in the vice, then the jaws of the vice should be covered with a soft material like sponge, rubber, felt or old rags.

**Obeche** (West Africa)   A smooth, yellow, inexpensive veneer, often used for wasters, backing, and compensating veneers.

**Off-cuts**   Bits and pieces of scrap wood and veneer left over from other projects. Save these for small jobs and try-outs; store them in labeled envelopes.

**PVA Glue**   Polyvinyl acetate adhesive; best for marquetry use because it comes in squeezy, easy-to-use containers and it is ready to use. However, waterbased PVA is not suitable for marquetries that will be left in damp conditions.

**Padouk** (Africa/Andaman Islands)   A rich, brilliantly-colored orange/red veneer, with an open grain and a slightly oily surface. Width 6—12 inches.

**Parquetry**   A decorative form of geometrical marquetry whereby veneers are variously cut and worked in jigs so as to create tessellating designs and motifs.

**Peartree** (Europe)   A delicate, pink, plain-textured, easy-to-use veneer; good for small intricate details and features. Width 6—12 inches.

**Pencils and Pencil-press Transferring**   Use a soft 2B for designing and tracing, and a hard 3H for pencil-press transferring. Trace the design with a 2B pencil, hinge-tape the tracing to the veneer, and then go over the drawn lines with a hard pencil.

**Piercing Saw**   A small frame saw, sometimes called a jeweler's saw and very much like a coping or fret saw. The frame can be adjusted to size to use short broken-blade lengths and very fine blades (FIG. G-9).

**Pins**  In the context of this book, pins or small nails are used to hold small pieces of veneer together. Use small brass or stainless steel pins.

**Plug Cutter**  A drill-like tool that bores out short dowels or plugs of wood. Plug cutters are designed so the resultant plugs exactly match up with standard drill sizes.

**Plywood or Multicore Ply**  When you are making boxes, base boards, and ground works with plywood, always use a close-grained, white, smooth-faced, best quality type that is made up from layers that are about $1/16$-inch thick. In use, multicore plywood can easily be cut and worked with all faces and edges being smooth and even.

**Prepared Wood**  Wood that has been planed and cut to a standard size.

**Press**  A press might be anything from complicated boards, battens, and G-clamp assembly to a board and a pile of bricks. Always bear in mind when you are sandwiching the workpiece prior to clamping, that the glue will ooze and spread. Therefore, only allow plastic sheet to come into contact with the workpiece.

**G-9**  As the piercing saw grips the blade ends, the fine blades can be passed through small pilot holes when cutting delicate middle windows and multi-layer veneers.

**Profiles**   In the context of this book, any cutout, cross-section, drawn shape, or flat fretted form.

**Prototype Design**   A working try-out design made prior to the project. If you have doubts as to whether or not the project will work, or if you are making modifications, then it's best to make a prototype design.

**Purpleheart** (Central America)   A beautiful medium- to dark-purple veneer. The color darkens as the veneer ages. Width 6–10 inches.

**Roller**   We recommend, when hot-iron pressing, the use of a rubber wallpaper seam roller or a small printing roller.

**Rubber Mat**   A good sheet material to use when pressing. Slide 1/16-inch-thick rubber mat between the workpiece and the clamping boards.

**Rubbing Down**   The process of working through the graded garnet papers from roughest to finest and sanding the wood down to a smooth finish. After using the garnet papers, rub the workpiece over with a slightly dampened cloth to remove all sanding dust.

**Sand-scorching**   Sand-scorching or sand shading is a picture- and pattern-making technique in which veneers are toned to create shaded, three-dimensional effects. Clean, fine, silver sand is heated and veneers are dipped for about five to six seconds until the required degree of toning has been achieved.

**Sapele** (West Africa)   A reddish-brown, easy-to-work soft veneer. It has warm toned pencil stripes. Width 8–12 inches.

**Satinwood** (Ceylon)   A yellow-gold veneer with a mottled figure and a lustrous sheen. Width 6–12 inches.

**Saws and Sawing**   Although we use many saw types, if you had to make do with just two saws, go for a tenon saw and a fretsaw.

**Scalpel**   A good quality, fine-bladed, razor-sharp scalpel and a plentiful supply of spare blades are a must. We use No. 11 surgical steel blades.

**Scraper**   A steel blade, the edges of which are slightly rounded and then burred with a file.

**Scroll Saw**   An electric scroll saw is one of those tools that you can easily do without, but once used, there is no going back. We use a Hegner saw.

**Sealers**   Used to provide a base coat for the varnish or polish. They can be applied with a brush or a rag (FIG. G-10).

**Set Square**   (try square). Used to test work for straightness or for 90° angles. Get one with a wooden stock and a metal blade.

**Straight Saws**   A straight-bladed, fine-toothed woodworking saw. We use a gents and a tenon.

**Stringer**   A plain, narrow strip or band of dark or light contrasting veneer, as might be inset between a picture and its border or frame.

**Sycamore** (England/USA)   A creamy-white, easy-to-use veneer, good for ground and waster sheets. Width 6–12 inches.

**Tracing Paper** (drafting paper)   A strong see-through paper used to transfer the master design to the workpiece.

**Varnishing Area**   It's best to varnish or polish in an area outside the main workshop. Spend time carefully setting out your varnish and materials, and generally see to it that the area is clean, dry, and free from dust.

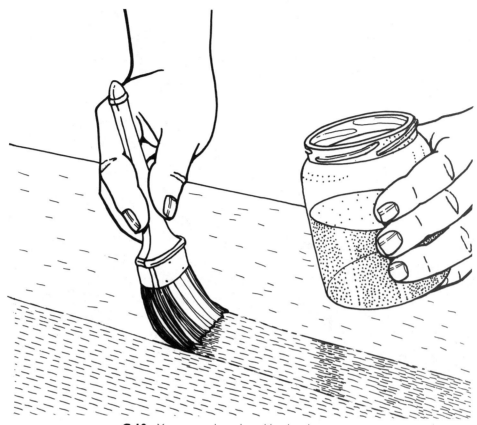

**G-10**   You can apply sealer with a brush or a rag.

**Veneer**   Thin slices of fancy-figured or exotic wood used to cover a base or ground wood. Veneers are used variously to construct, conceal, and embellish. Veneers are used in marquetry and inlay as both surface and inset decoration.

**Vice**   A bench-mounted screw clamp used for holding and securing wood while it is being worked.

**Waster**   A sheet of veneer on which the design is drawn out. Using the window technique, parts of the design are cut away and these are then filled in with choice woods. Progressively, areas are cut away and replaced, until the original waster sheet of veneer only forms a small part of the design, or has been replaced altogether.

**Wax**   Wax used to finish, polish or burnish wood. We use a clear beeswax.

**Window Method**   In the context of this book, the window method is the primary technique used for constructing and laying picture marquetry. First, the design is drawn out on a waster sheet of veneer, and selected parts of the design, or "windows" are cut away from the waster. Choice sheets of veneer are then positioned under the windows so that the color and figure are shown to best advantage (FIG. G-11). The shape of the hole is marked through to the selected

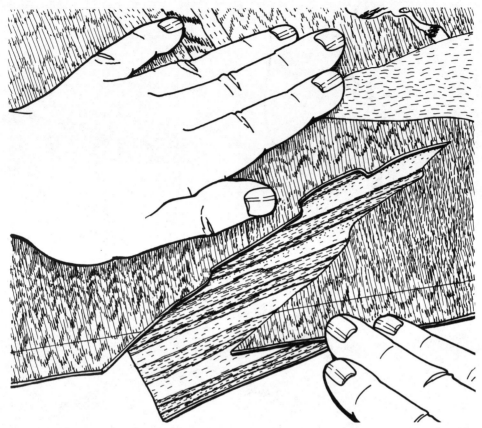

**G-11** Position the choice veneer under the window and mark the shape of the hole through to the veneer.

veneer and cut to fit the window. Then the cutout is pressed back into the hole and fitted with a tab of masking tape.

**Workbench**   In a marquetry and inlay context, a workbench might be anything from a table out in the garage to a woodworker's bench complete with a vice. Ideally, the surface needs to be strong, clean, stable, and not too precious.

**Working Drawings**   (See **gridded working drawing**).

**Working Face**   The best side of the workpiece; the side that shows; the important face.

**Work-out Paper**   Rough paper on which all the pre-project notes, details, and sketches are worked out.

# Decorating a table mat with a patchwork parquetry design

**S**quares, checkerboard counterchanges, triangles, diamonds, lozenges, chevrons and zigzags—they are all beautiful! Well, perhaps I should say that they are all beautiful if you like straight lines, math, compass work and geometry.

Parquetry is the art and craft of the straight line. The mounting, setting and gluing techniques are the same as in marquetry, but while marquetry involves naturalistic, impressionistic, and pattern imagery, parquetry concentrates entirely on straight lines and geometrical patterns. Many marquetarians think of parquetry as being tedious and unadventurous, but not a bit of it. Parquetry is a technique that requires a great deal of skill, ingenuity, and imagination. Many American and European marquetarians think of parquetry as being similar to fabric patchwork, and this is a good comparison.

If you like geometry, order, logic, and rhythm, then this is the project for you.

## CONSIDERING THE DESIGN

Have a good long look at the project picture and working drawings and see how, at a grid scale of four squares to 1 inch, the diamond shapes that make up the traditional cubes design have a side measurement of exactly 1 inch (FIGS. 1-1 and 1-2). Note the 60/30° structure of the diamond, and see how it can be cut and worked from a 7/8-inch-wide veneer strip. Study the jig design and see how it can be quickly made with a few strips of masking tape. Note that the safety ruler and veneer channels cross at a precise 30/60° "Z" angle.

Cutting the diamonds is simple enough. Slide a 7/8-inch-wide strip of veneer into the jig channel and bridge the strip with the safety ruler. Make sure that both the strip and the ruler are held firm, and then cut across the veneer. If you then slide the strip along some, so that the angled end is butted into the angled end of the channel, and then repeat the procedure, you finish up with a beautifully angled diamond. The secret of success is in the jig. The angles must be 30/60°— no more or less.

Have a look at the cube design and see how it needs to be made up from three different veneer colors. Best go for straight grained, easy-to-cut woods like Afri-

**1-1** Project picture. The scale is four grid squares to 1 inch. Traditional "cube" parquetry—made up from 60/30° diamonds—note how the three veneer types run out from a six pointed star design.

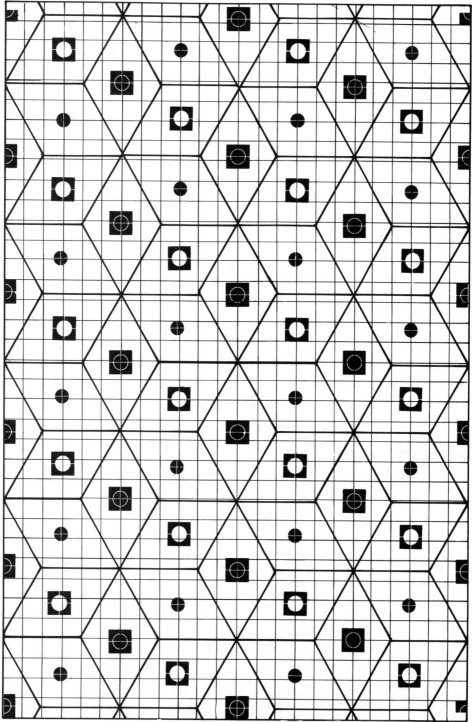

**1-2** Working drawing. The scale is four grid squares to 1 inch. Note the 1-inch side measurement of the diamonds.

can walnut, padouk, and cedar of Lebanon. Note that the three symbols on the working drawing represent the three veneer colors.

## TOOLS AND MATERIALS

In addition to the items listed on p. xi, you will need:
- A 1/4-inch-thick plywood table mat, size to suit.
- Three pieces of veneer at 18 × 6 inches.
- A sheet of thermoplastic gluefilm to suit your chosen mat.
- A small tin of filler.
- A 60/30° plastic or metal set square—the bigger the better.
- An electric flat iron.
- A tin of tung oil.

## THE PROJECT

Study the working drawing again and note how important it is that the 60/30° angles be worked with care and precision, and then use your masking tape and cutting board to make a diamond jig (FIG. 1-3). Set two parallel tapes 7/8 inch apart for the veneer channel. Have the diamond shape carefully angled and stopped so that the diamond sides measure 1 inch.

When you have made the jig, have a trial work-out with a sheet of thin scrap card. Tape the diamonds together and hold the sheet up to the light to check joints. If there are any problems, adjust the jig accordingly. Once you have achieved a good jig, double the masking tape thickness to make well-stepped veneer and ruler stops.

With the jig made and checked, take one or other of the veneers and use the measure, straightedge, and scalpel to cut off a 7/8-inch-wide strip. Slide the veneer into the jig and push the end hard up against the end-stop. Bridge the strip with the safety ruler and cut through the veneer with several passes of the knife. This will give you your first 30/60° angle (FIG. 1-4). Remove the waste piece, slide the angled end against the end stop, and repeat the cutting action. When you are cutting, make sure you run the blade hard up against the rule.

Continue pushing the strip along the jig channel until it is hard up against the end-stop, aligning the ruler with the various stops, and then slicing off another diamond motif. You need an equal number of light-, medium-and dark-colored diamonds.

When you think you have cut enough pieces to cover the table mat with a generous overlap, have another look at the working drawing design, and then assemble the pieces, best-face-up, on the work surface. Hold each diamond shape against its neighbor to make sure they are well aligned. Then fix the points with small tabs of masking tape. All the fixing is done on the best face (FIG. 1-5, top).

Of course, you want to aim for a perfect fit, but as it's almost impossible to achieve perfection, so be prepared for a deal of swapping around and refitting. When you have fiddled, chopped, and changed the shapes around for best effect, run strips of masking tape along the seams and remove the temporary tabs of tape (FIG. 1-5, bottom).

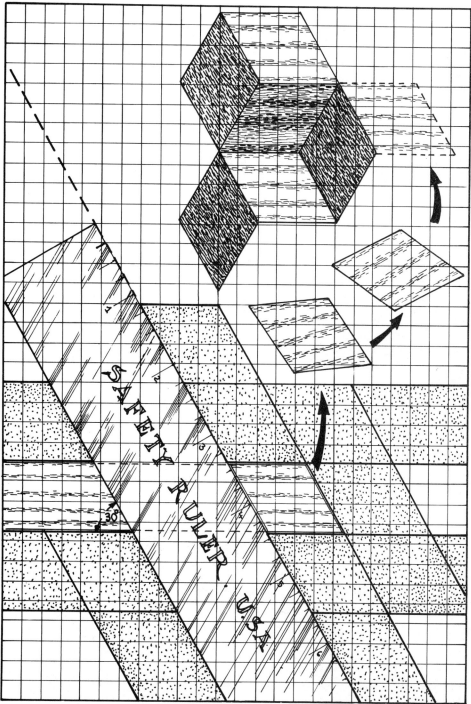

**I-3**  Cutting grid/jig. The scale is four grid squares to I inch. The ⁷/₈-inch-wide strip is set in the jig channel, and the safety ruler is butted hard up against the masking tape stops.

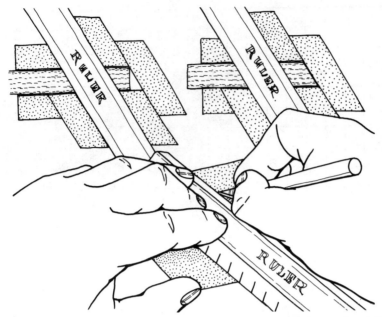

**I-4** Cut off the first 30°/60° angle and remove the piece of square-ended waste (top left). Repeat the cutting action to achieve the first diamond shaped motif (top right). Make sure that you run the blade hard up against the rule (bottom).

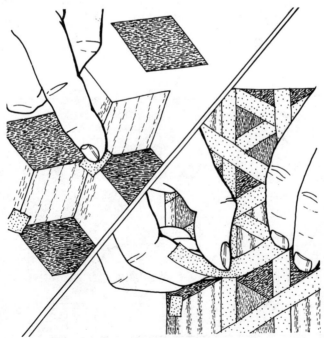

**I-5** Fix the points of the diamonds together with masking tape (top), running the tape along the seams, and remove the temporary tape (bottom).

Turn the taped design over so that its best face is down, and carefully ease a small amount of filler into any joints you think are slightly gappy or less than perfect. Use as small amount of filler as possible and clean off the excess. This done, cut a sheet of gluefilm to fit the plywood mat, clean up the mess and clutter, and switch the electric iron on to medium. Place the gluefilm paper-side-up on the plywood mat base or groundwork, and smooth it over with the hot iron (FIG. 1-6, top).

When the film has cooled, carefully peel off the backing paper and lay the veneer design in position, making sure that the design slightly overlaps and is square with the plywood base. Cover the veneer with the backing paper to protect it from scorching, and work the hot iron slowly back and forth over the surface until all the glue has melted (FIG. 1-6, bottom). Remove the backing paper, turn the whole work over, and use a scalpel to trim off surplus veneer. Hold the knife blade hard up against the ply edge.

Carefully ease off the masking tape and use a spirit-damped cloth to remove all traces of sticky residue. Use the graded glass/garnet paper to rub the edges and

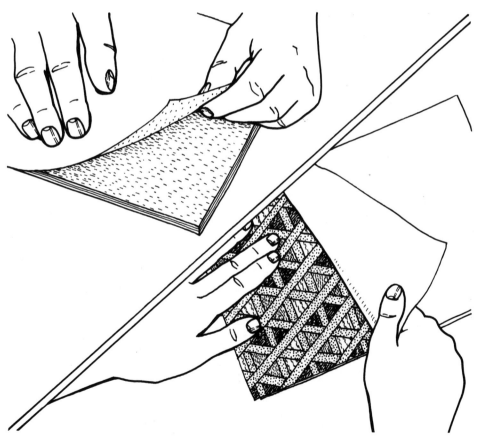

**1-6** Place the gluefilm paper-side-up on the plywood mat (top), and cover the veneer with backing paper to protect it from scorching (bottom).

face down to a perfect smooth finish. Then wipe away the dust and burnish the work with a small amount of tung oil.

## HINTS

It is vital that you spend time getting the jig just right. Double check angles, make sure that various masking tape stops are accurately placed and well stepped.

When you are cutting the veneer, don't try to cut through it at a single stroke. Rather, cut it with three or four well-placed strokes.

You will almost certainly have to swap and change the shapes around for best fit. Veneers are pliable, so you will be able to close small gaps when you apply heat and pressure.

In this instance, have the plywood edges plain or stained black. You might have a plain veneer on the back of the mat.

# 2

# Decorating a tray with floral marquetry

**P**icture a warm summer afternoon, a blue sky, the soft flitter of butterflies, and a nice comfortable chair in the shade of an old apple tree—wonderful! What could be better? Well, for our money at least, we would like to complete the picture by painting in a table and a tray all set for afternoon tea. And no doubt you have guessed already that we would also like the tray to be decorated with a traditional floral marquetry design.

OK, so it's not always possible to conjure up beautiful weather, green lawns and all the rest—but the tray we can manage. Trays and tabletops pose a particularly interesting problem in that the design will be seen from many angles. For this reason, one might choose to work a circular motif, a hexagonal design, or a quartered design, or a pattern that repeats itself all around the tray. In this instance, however, you will work a simple, mirror-image motif on a center line.

Although the finished product looks like a mirror image, because it is worked using the "window" method, the two designs and all the elements are actually cut and fitted individually. The window method makes it possible to build into the design a subtle flow and delicacy, with all the seemingly identical motifs and details being ever so slightly different. Therefore, when you come to cutting the individual windows that make up the Chinese lantern-shaped flowers, you will be able to angle a choice piece of veneer this way and that, until the flow of the grain perfectly fits the shape and form of the flower. If you are looking to have a special afternoon tea on the lawn, maybe this is the project for you!

## CONSIDERING THE PROJECT

Have a good look at the project picture and the working drawing (FIGS. 2-1 and 2-2), and see how the design relates to the shape of the tray. Note the way the soft, downward flow of the leaves at the center of the design makes for a strong central motif. The design draws inspiration from an early nineteenth century art nouveau stencilled motif. Note the way the stems entwine and the way the teardrop shapes within the lanterns curl and point.

The lanterns need to be a strong orange color, so we have chosen to use padouk—a beautiful, grainy, oily, orange wood, just perfect for the Chinese lantern imagery, although it can be tricky to cut. For the leaves, we have chosen to use shades of harewood. By careful use and selection of various green/gray types,

**2-1** Project picture. The scale is three grid squares to 2 inches. Note how the design has been quartered and mirror-imaged.

**2-2** Working drawing. The scale is three grid squares to 2 inches.

it is possible to achieve the necessary light- and dark-shaded leaf effects. As for the background, we have chosen pearwood because of its soft pink/cream color, and its easy-to-cut characteristics.

Note that the vein lines are created by changing textures and colors of neighboring butt-jointed veneers. See also how the main black stems are best cut and worked in short lengths—decide how you want the grain to go, decide where you want the joints to be, and then adjust the working order accordingly.

## TOOLS AND MATERIALS

In addition to the items listed on p. xi, you will need:
- A flat plywood tray to cover, stripped of all edges and fittings, measuring 16 × 24 inches.
- Enough pearwood veneer to cover the tray. Allow for a generous overlap.
- A quantity of orange padouk for the lanterns.
- A small quantity of harewood for the leaves in several shades from green to gray.
- A small amount of dyed black sycamore for the main stems.
- A sheet of tracing paper at $16^1/2 \times 12^1/2$ inches.
- A sheet of carbon paper at 16 × 12 inches.
- A pack of fine stainless steel dressmakers pins.
- A pair of clamping boards larger than the tray.
- A couple of large sheets of plastic film.
- Four clamping battens.
- Four G-clamps/G-cramps.
- A tin of polyurethane varnish.
- A brush.
- A stack of newspaper.

## THE PROJECT

Once you have a clear understanding of just how the project needs to be worked, take a good full-size tracing of the half-tray design (FIG. 2-2). Trim, cut, fit and tape the four sheets of pearwood so that you have two half-tray sheets at $12^1/2 \times 16^1/2$ inches. Have the grain running the lengths of the tray, through the width of $12^1/2$- × $16^1/2$-inch half-tray sheets. The extra $1/2$ inch allows for a trim-back overlap.

Take the half-tray tracing and tape it hinge-like to the top edge of the pearwood veneer (FIG. 2-3, top). Sandwich the carbon paper between the tracing and the veneer, and pencil-press transfer the traced image through to the wood (FIG. 2-3, bottom).

Having transferred the lines of the design, hinge the tracing out of the way, remove the carbon paper, support the veneer on the cutting mat, and then set about cutting out one or other of the peardrop shapes that will make up the Chinese lanterns. Use a series of delicate, little-by-little strokes to cut away the part motif until you are left with a clean-edged hole, or window.

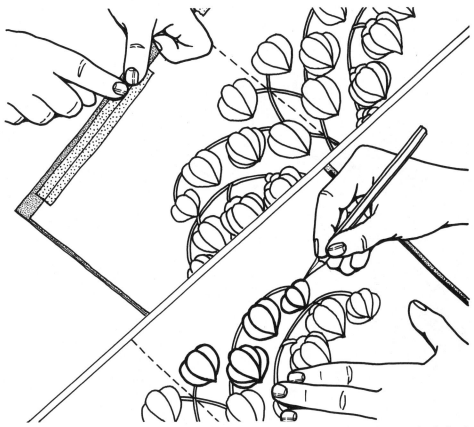

**2-3** Take the half-tray tracing and hinge-tape it to the top edge of the pearwood veneer (top). Sandwich the carbon paper between the tracing and the veneer and pencil-press transfer the traced lines (bottom).

Now take a sheet of choice padouk and slide it behind the window. Arrange it for best effect and pin it into place, making sure that the pins are positioned in an area that is to be wasted (FIG. 2-4, top). Run the point of the scalpel blade several times around the inside edge of the window. Don't try to cut through; just make sure that the outline is clearly established.

Remove the veneer from behind the window and set about cutting out the motif. Make several passes with the scalpel, and, if necessary, support the cut-out with temporary reinforcing strips of masking tape on the back of the veneer (FIG. 2-4, bottom).

When you have trimmed the cut-out to a perfect fit, pop it into its window and hold it in place with small tabs of masking tape on the best/front face of the design. Continue working across the design until all the motif windows have been replaced with choice veneers. Note how, in many instances, one window leads directly into the next with neighboring holes sharing the same part-profile or line of cut.

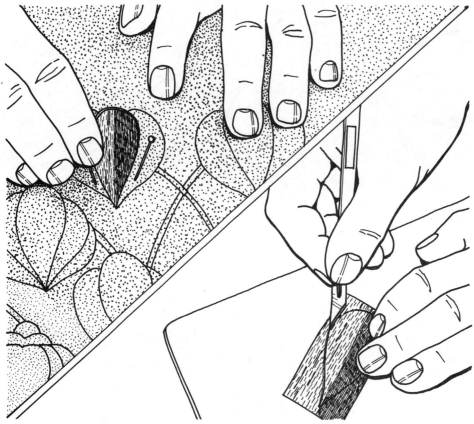

**2-4** Slide the padouk veneer behind the window and arrange it for best grain effect. Make sure that the pins are positioned in an area that is to be wasted (top). Cut through the veneer by making several passes with the scalpel (bottom).

When you have completed the design by repeating the procedure to work the other side of the mirrored design, remove all the tabs of tape. Replace these with side-by-side strips of tape that run the full length of the tray, placing the tape on the best face.

When you have achieved what you consider is a well-fitted and fixed design, set out the prepared plywood tray with all edge fittings removed. Because the PVA glue you will use next is water-based and water causes veneer to curl, give the plywood tray base a generous coating of adhesive (FIG. 2-5, top).

Place the marquetry piece best-face-down on the clean work surface and pencil in small guidelines to help with the tray placement. Wait about ten minutes for the glue to go tacky, then flip the tray over and set it glue-side-down on the marquetry veneer. Make sure the veneer is perfectly aligned and then clamp it. The clamping sandwich order is: clamping battens, clamping board, newspaper, plastic sheet, the marquetry piece, plastic sheet, newspaper, clamping board, and clamping battens (FIG. 2-5, bottom).

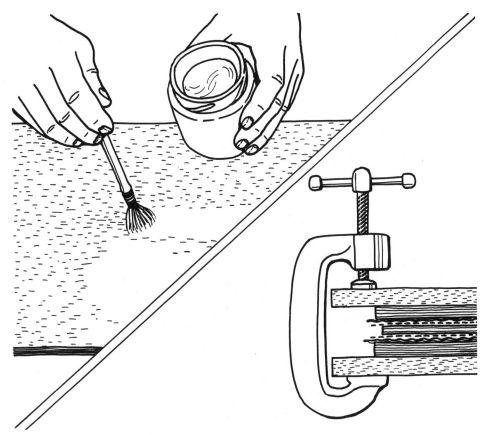

**2-5** Give the plywood tray base a generous coating of adhesive (top). Make sure all pieces are sandwiched and held securely by the clamps (bottom).

When the glue has dried, remove the work from the clamps and set it tape-side-up on the work surface. One piece at a time, carefully peel back the tape and ease it away from the veneer. NOTE: If you try to rip the tape off in one great heave, you will damage the face of the work (FIG. 2-6).

Use a turpentine-damped cloth and a scraper to remove all traces of masking tape. Flip the tray best-face-down and use a knife to trim off the waste overlap. Then rub the work down with the block and the graded sand/garnet paper. Gradually work through the papers from coarse to fine, doing the best face and edges.

Finally, when the work is smooth to the touch, wipe away all traces of dust. Lay on at least two coats of polyurethane varnish and reassemble the tray edges and fittings. Allow 6–12 hours between varnish coats.

## HINTS

When you are cutting and fitting the four pieces of pearwood veneer that make up the background, make sure that the edges are perfectly butt-jointed.

You could choose a background veneer that has a subtle grain and redesign

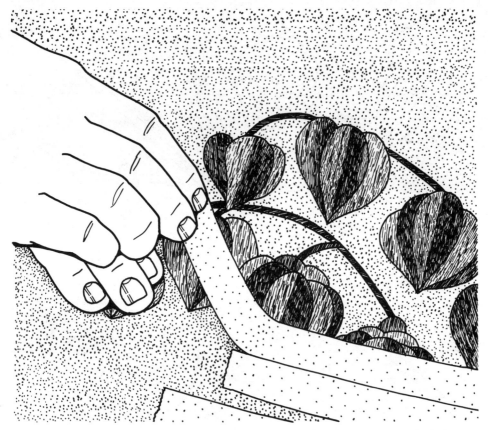

**2-6** When you remove the tape, peel and ease it away in little-by-little stages so you don't damage the workpiece.

the four sections that make up the background so that they "diamond match" (See clock project, #18).

Padouk can be brittle, hard, and thick, so reinforce it with strips of masking tape. If you are a beginner, you could go for a straight grained easy-to-work, veneer like dyed sycamore, Purpleheart, or Virginian pencil cedar.

Be generous when you come to gluing, but not so generous that the glue oozes all over the work surface. Cover the work surface with newspaper.

When you are gluing and clamping up, make sure that the plastic sheet is always between the workpiece and the newspaper. Newsprint ink can stain delicate veneers.

# Making a games board

**A** dark and dreary winter evening, the curtains drawn, a roaring fire in the hearth, a glass of your favorite tipple, a wedge of homemade cake, a piece of soft music, a special friend by your side, and a game of chess, checkers, or backgammon on the go . . . Sounds great, doesn't it?

Traditional board games are a joy—fast and furious, while at the same time calming and contemplative. But to be playing the game on a beautiful board you have made with your own two hands is surely the gilt on the gingerbread.

## CONSIDERING THE PROJECT

Have a good, long look at the project picture and the working drawings (FIGS. 3-1, 3-2, and 3-3) and see how the project relates to three games. On one side of the board is 64 squares for checkers or chess, and on the other side is the backgammon layout with the long, zigzag fingers. Both designs call for a fair amount of precise knife work. The checkers design is worked using the parquetry strip method, while the backgammon layout is worked using the window technique. Although these techniques are a bit tricky, if you take it nice and easy and one step at a time, you won't go far wrong.

## TOOLS AND MATERIALS

In addition to the items listed on p. xi, you need:
- A sheet of $1/2$-inch-thick plywood at 14 × 16 inches.
- Sixteen strips of veneer at $1^3/8$ inches wide × 12 inches long, for the checkers face—eight dark and eight light. Go for easy-to-cut woods like dark mahogany, light boxwood and light sycamore.
- Four light colored veneer strips at $1/8$ inch wide × 12 inches long, for the checker board fillets.
- Two strips of dark-colored veneer at about $16^1/2$ inches long and 2 inches wide, for the long side borders—for the checkers board.
- Two strips of dark-colored veneer at about 14 inches long and 3 inches wide, for the short-side, crossband borders—for the checkers board. Note that the grain must go across the width of the strips.
- Two sheets of white veneer at about 8 × 14 inches for the main playing face of the backgammon board.
- Two sheets of veneer at about 5 × 12 inches for the triangles, one yellow and one brown, for the backgammon board.

**3-1** Project picture. The project relates to three games—checkers, chess, and backgammon.

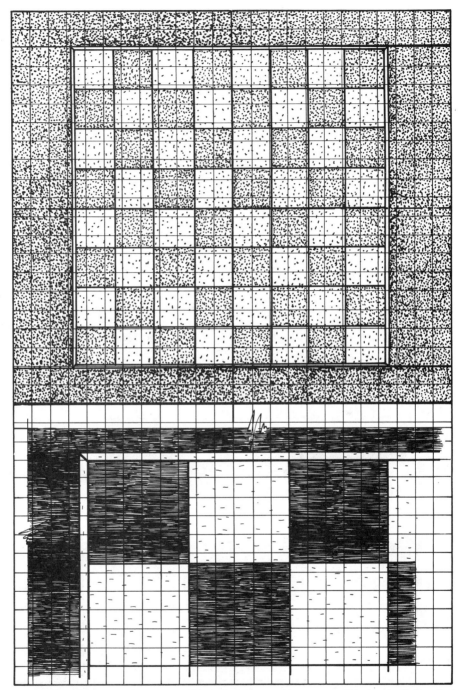

**3-2** Working drawing—checker board. The scale is three grid squares to 2 inches (top). Detail: the scale is about four grid squares to 1 inch. Note the light-dark-light counterchange and the direction of the grain (bottom).

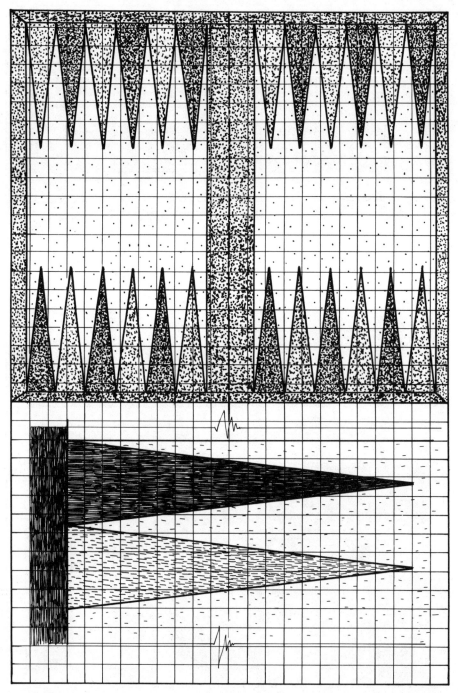

**3-3** Working drawing—backgammon board, the scale is three grid squares to 2 inches (top). Detail: the scale is about four grid squares to 1 inch. Note the light-dark-light counterchange and the direction of the grain (bottom).

- A brown strip at about 1½ × 14 inches for the central strip of the backgammon board.
- A good selection of strips for the board edges.
- A board-size sheet of carbon paper.
- A set square.
- A clamping board.
- A sheet of plastic.
- A tin of clear yacht varnish.

## THE PROJECT

### Making the checkers board face

Take nine strips of 1³/₈-inch-wide veneer—five light and four dark—and put them side-by-side on the work surface so that the colors run light, dark, light, dark, etc. (FIG. 3-4, top). Being very careful to keep the veneers perfectly aligned, join them edge-to-edge with the masking tape. Start and finish with light strips until you have nine strips in all.

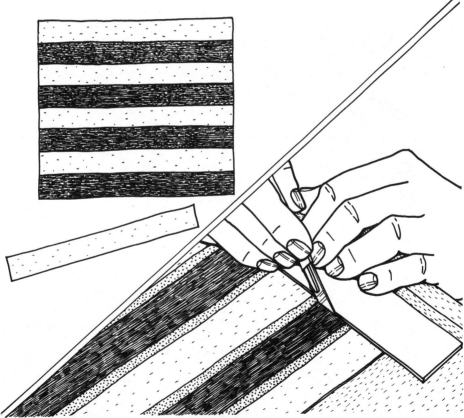

**3-4** Checkers board—set nine strips of 1³/₈-inch-wide veneer side by side and fix them with strips of masking tape (top). Use the safety ruler and the scalpel to cut off the 1³/₈-wide strips (bottom).

Take the cutting mat, the knife and the set square, and square off the assembly. Make sure that it is exactly 90°. Use the pencil, ruler and set square to mark out across the assembly eight 1³/₈-inch-wide strips. Make up a batten or masking tape jig and cut them off with the knife (FIG. 3-4, bottom).

When you have cut the eight strips, realign them side-by-side—only this time, move one to the left and one to the right down the assembly to achieve the characteristic checkered effect (FIG. 3-5, top). Fit and fix the strips with the masking tape and cut away the excess light-colored squares. Again, be sure the assembly is at a 90° angle.

Next, take the 64-square assembly and carefully frame and tape the ¹/₈-inch-wide white fillets around what is now the playing area, making sure the fillets cross at the corners. Support the workpiece on the cutting mat and snip through the two-thickness cross-over with the knife to achieve a 45° miter. Do this on all four corners (FIG. 3-5, bottom).

Fit the four border strips. Place the cross-grained or crossbanded strips on the playing ends, and the sides strips running along each side of the board. The

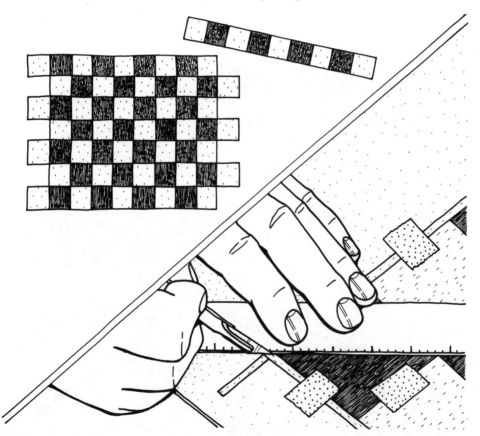

**3-5** Checkers board—rearrange the strips to achieve the checkered design and fix with strips of masking tape (top). Overlap the stringers and cut through the crossover to achieve the 45° miter (bottom).

crossbanded strips need to be set between the side strips. Make sure that the finished assembly is slightly larger than the board.

## Making the backgammon face

Put the checkerboard face to one side. Set out the two large sheets of white veneer so that the grain is nicely centered, matched and mirror-imaged. Slide the 1³/₈-inch-wide brown strip between the two sheets of white, and fit and fix with strips of masking tape (FIG. 3-6, top).

Trace off the backgammon design and use the carbon paper to pencil-press transfer the lines of the design through to the veneer. Make sure the lines are clear and accurate.

Look again at the project picture to verify the various veneer colors, and cut out one or other of the triangles, using the safety ruler and the scalpel. When you have cut out the triangular window, slide a selected piece of veneer behind the hole, move it around for best visual effect, and mark the shape through (FIG. 3-6,

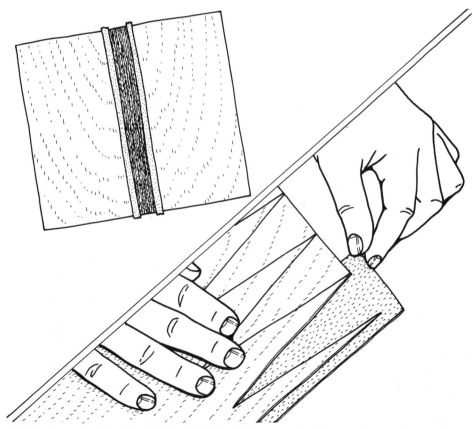

**3-6** Backgammon board—tape the 1³/₈-inch-wide brown strip between the two sheets of white (top). Cut out the triangular window and slide a choice piece of veneer behind the hole (bottom).

bottom). Cut, trim, fit and fix the triangle into the window and hold it in place with masking tape.

Continue cutting out the triangles, fitting alternate brown-yellow triangles, and fixing with masking tape until the design is complete. Double-check along the way with the project picture and the working drawing. Mark and fit the border strips. Overlap them at the corners and cut through the overlap, creating perfect 45° mitered corners.

With the backgammon layout well taped and set best-face-down on the work surface, spread the white PVA glue over one face of the baseboard. After about ten minutes, when the glue is tacky, flip over the baseboard and set it glue-side-down on the backgammon veneer assemble and apply pressure. Flip the board over and check the fit, then cover the veneer face with a plastic sheet and several layers of newspaper. Put it in a clamp or under a weighted board.

When the glue is dry, remove the plastic sheet and the newspaper and peel off the masking tape. Set the board face-down on a clean cutting board and trim off the overlaps of veneer waste (FIG. 3-7).

Continue working the backgammon assembly, the edge strips and the checkerboard assembly. When you come to fixing the edge strips, apply a small amount

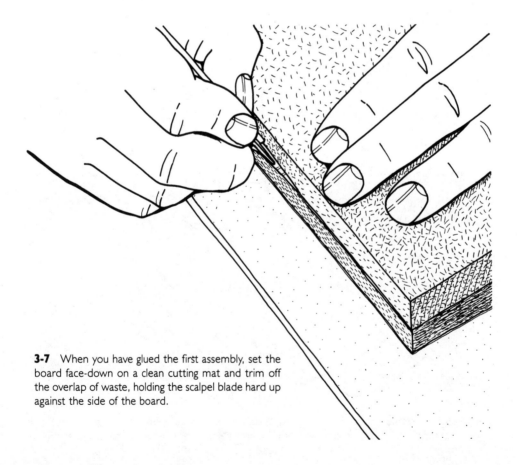

**3-7** When you have glued the first assembly, set the board face-down on a clean cutting mat and trim off the overlap of waste, holding the scalpel blade hard up against the side of the board.

of glue to opposite edges, and clamp or tape the oversize edge strips in place until the glue has set. Then trim off the overlaps.

Finally, when you have what you consider is a well-set-up board, rub all surfaces down to a good, smooth finish. Wipe away all traces of dust and glue, and lay on at least three coats of clear varnish. Let the varnish dry out between coats.

## HINTS

With a project of this nature, it is most important that the joints be tight and well set out, so work slowly and carefully. If you discover tape buildup after fixing the assembly, it's a good idea to peel off the tape and replace it with single strips.

Don't overdo the clamping. Make sure that the veneers stay well aligned.

Because both sides of the board are being worked, make an extra effort to keep the surfaces clean and free from debris.

# 4
# Making a marquetry mirror-image tray

Mirror-image marquetry is a wonderfully satisfying and complete technique. Rather like boulle work, it is a positive/negative method that involves cutting two veneers at the same time and then swapping over cut pieces so as to make two identical counterchange designs. That said, mirror-image marquetry takes the counterchange idea one step further. Not only are the cutouts swapped over, they are also changed over so that both the positive and the negative images share the same baseline. In this way, half of the design looks to be a direct mirror-image reflection of the other.

Boats on lakes, swans on ponds, houses, mountains, and trees reflected in still waters—and, of course, a cat looking at his reflection in a puddle of water. If you enjoy traditional picture marquetry, this is the project for you.

## CONSIDERING THE PROJECT

Cats, cats, cats! White cats, black cats, ginger cats, tortoiseshells, tabbies, Persians, calico cats, marmalades and Siamese—there's no denying that cats are uniquely delightful creatures. Have a look at the project picture and the working drawing (FIGS. 4-1 and 4-2), and see how the cat image is used to great effect in this curious mirror-image design. A white cat with a black ear looking at a reflection of a black cat with a white ear—or maybe it's a white cat with a black ear looking at a reflection of a black cat with a white ear! See what we mean about curious?

All that apart, note that the working drawing shows two grid squares to 1 inch and the tray measures about 12 inches in diameter. See also how the tray edge is built up and laminated out of several thin veneer strip layers. In addition, this project calls for an electric jigsaw/scroll saw—we use a Hegner fitted with superfine piercing saw blades.

Finally, study the details and see how the various cutouts are swapped over. The main cat profiles are changed, then the ears, and then the eyes. It's all very straightforward.

## TOOLS AND MATERIALS

In addition to the items listed on p. xi, you need:
- A sheet of good quality, 1/4-inch-thick plywood at about $12^{1}/2 \times 12^{1}/2$ inches square.

**4-1** Project picture. Note how the design is worked from two contrasting sheets of veneer, and how the cutouts have been counterchanged.

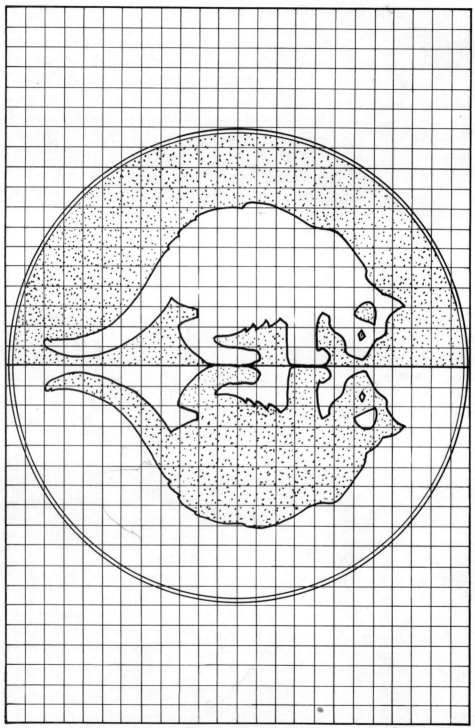

**4-2** Working drawing. The scale is about two grid squares to 1 inch.

- Two sheets of veneer at about 12½ × 6½ inches. You need contrasting veneers; we use pommelle and aspen.
- Two sheets of thin waster ply at 12½ × 6½ inches.
- Six veneer strips at ¾ inches wide and 36 inches long for the tray edge.
- A sheet of tracing paper.
- A hand drill and a small needle bit.
- The use of an electric fretsaw/scroll saw; we use a Hegner.
- A pack of medium saw blades.
- A pack of fine-tooth piercing or jeweler's blades; we use ⁴/o and ²/o sizes.
- A tin of polyurethane varnish.

## THE PROJECT

Take the 12½- × 12½-inch-square sheet of ¼-inch-thick plywood, and use the pencil and ruler to draw crossed diagonals to fix the center. With the compass set to a radius of 6 inches, spike the compass point on the center and scribe out a 12-inch-diameter circle.

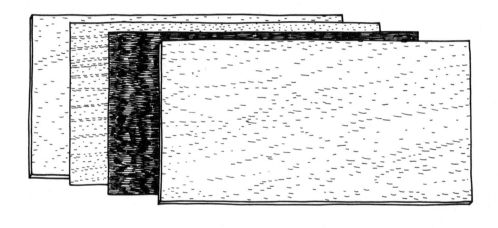

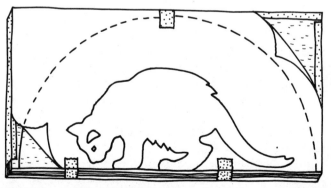

**4-3** Sandwich the sheets of veneer between the two sheets of plywood (top). Tape the traced design onto the sandwich so that the bottom edge is perfectly aligned (bottom).

Fit a medium blade in the scroll saw and cut out the 12-inch-diameter plywood disc. Keep the line of cut just to the outside of the drawn line, and aim to cut a cleanedged circle. You can sand back to the drawn line.

Take the two sheets of veneer and the two sheets of waster ply and sandwich them up—ply, light veneer, dark veneer and ply. Make sure the edges are clean and square (FIG. 4-3, top). Strap up the whole sandwich with masking tape, two $6^1/2$-inch side edges and on one long $12^1/2$-inch edge.

With the compass set to a radius of $6^1/8$ inches, spike the compass point on the middle center of the bottom untaped edge, and scribe a $12^1/4$-diameter half-circle. Trace off the project picture, with the tracing paper square on the bottom untaped edge of the sandwiched veneer. Pencil-press transfer the traced line through to the top-most sheet of ply (FIG. 4-3, bottom).

Fit the scroll saw with one of the fine piercing blades, and set the veneer/ply sandwich tracing-face up and waster side down. Switch on the scroll saw; have the teeth of the saw pointing down toward the work.

Starting with one of the little islands, like say the cats eye, drill a small pilot hole somewhere along the line of cut. Unhitch the blade from the saw frame and pass it through the hole. Then fit and retension the blade, and continue to saw. Work at an easy, slow pace, staying with the drawn line, and presenting the saw blade with the line of next cut (FIG. 4-4). Continue until all the parts that make up the design have been carefully fretted out.

When all the parts have been cut and worked, remove the pieces of waste or support ply and set out the ten cutouts. You should have two background half-circles, two cat profiles, two under-leg pieces, two eyes and two ears.

Set the cutouts best-face-up on the work surface and relocate the various pieces. Make the total circle with the two half-circles, counterchange the cat profiles so that light is in dark and dark within light, and then counterchange the ears and the eyes. Make sure all the spaces between the pieces are well balanced. When you are happy with the overall arrangement, tape the assembly secure (FIG. 4-5, top).

Flip the assembly best-face-down, smear white PVA adhesive over the plywood tray circle, and wait a short while for the glue to become tacky. Then set the plywood disc down on the marquetry assembly and place it under a weighted board. Make sure that there is a small, even band of overlap all around the disc.

When the glue is dry, set the board veneer-side-down on the cutting board and carefully cut away the overlap of waste with the scapel. Put the tray in the jaws of a padded vice and use garnet/glass paper and a cork block to finish the tray edge, using your fingertips to align the block (FIG. 4-5, bottom).

Now comes the tricky part. Take one of the long, thin strips for the tray edge and cut one end square. Wrap the strip around the disc so that the ends overlap and pull the strip tight around the edge of the tray. Mark for an exact butt-edge fit and cut the strip to size.

Smear a small amount of PVA around the edge of the board and allow the glue to go tacky. Then fit the strip around the edge and tape it in place. Make sure that there is a slight overlap on the underside of the tray (FIG. 4-6).

After gluing the first strip, remove the tape, cut the second strip to fit the

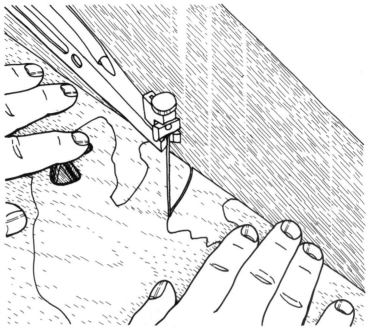

**4-4** Hold the workpiece firmly flat on the cutting table and keep the wood moving so that the blade is always presented with the line of next cut.

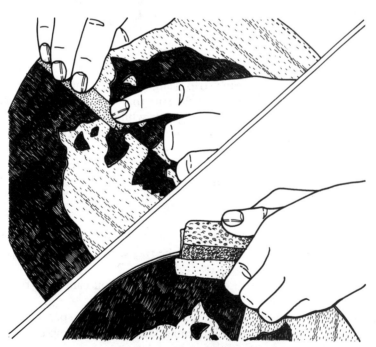

**4-5** Use tabs of masking tape to hold the pieces secure and in place (top). Use garnet paper and a cork sanding block to rub down the edges of the tray (bottom).

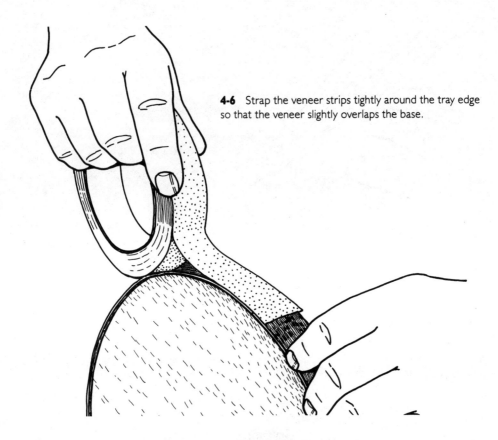

**4-6** Strap the veneer strips tightly around the tray edge so that the veneer slightly overlaps the base.

slightly increased circumference, and then repeat the procedure. Don't try to cut the six strips all at once because each strip is slightly longer than the one before it. When you are fitting successive strips, make sure that the joints are well staggered and that each strip is held firmly to its neighbor while the glue sets.

Finally, when all six strips have been fitted, remove all traces of masking tape and rub the surfaces and edges down with the graded sandpaper. Level off the underside strip edge so that it is flush with the underside of the tray, and lay on a couple of coats of polyurethane varnish.

## HINTS

If you want to make a real exhibition piece, or if you are worried about the tray warping, you could cover the underside of the tray with a sheet of compensating veneer.

If you can't get access to an electric scroll saw, you can use a fretsaw or a piercing saw.

When you are setting the cutouts, make sure that all the spaces made by the saw cut between the cutouts are well balanced. Don't, for example, push the cat profile hard up against one side of the surround.

You can buy a tray kit and redesign the project to fit the tray.

# 5

# Making a marquetry picture

**W**indow marquetry is wonderfully easy—a sharp craft knife, a pack of veneers, a roll of low-tack masking tape, and you're off. It really is perfect for beginners. Of course, you do need to invest in one or two small basic items—tracing paper, carbon paper, pencils and the like—but that said, the knifeworked window method is one of the best ways to get involved in marquetry. If you are looking for a swift, easy, low-cost way into the craft, then this is the project for you.

The window method involves tracing the design, pencil-press transferring the traced design through to a *waster*, or sheet of sacrificial, easy-to-cut veneer. Then you cut away various elements, or *windows* of the design, and replace the windows with selected veneers of your choice.

Because you are working in small steps, you are able to correct mistakes and/ or make alterations as you go along. In addition, the window method allows you to play with the veneers—study the colors, the character of the veneer, and the direction and run of the grain. And you can relate successive stages to the windows you have already built up (FIG. 5-1).

## CONSIDERING THE DESIGN

Before you rush off and start buying veneers, baseboards, and so on, it's always a good idea to spend some time studying the implications of the project. Note how this particular design relates to a nineteenth century Russian windmill. See also how the picture has been broken down into basic, easy-to-work shapes. Study all the working details and decide just how you want your own marquetry to be (FIGS. 5-1 and 5-2). For example, do you want to change the scale and have the picture larger or smaller? Or do you want to shift the emphasis and have the windmill fill the whole of the picture? Do you like the idea of the "window" method, but want to change the theme and have a cottage rather than a windmill? These are all points to consider.

Finally, have another good look at the gridded working drawings, and see how, at a scale of four grid squares to 1 inch, the picture measures 6 × 9 inches. Note the number of windows and, consequentially, the number of veneer type possibilities (FIG. 5-2).

**5-1** Project picture. This particular design draws inspiration from a nineteenth century windmill picture. We have broken the picture down into easy-to-work shapes.

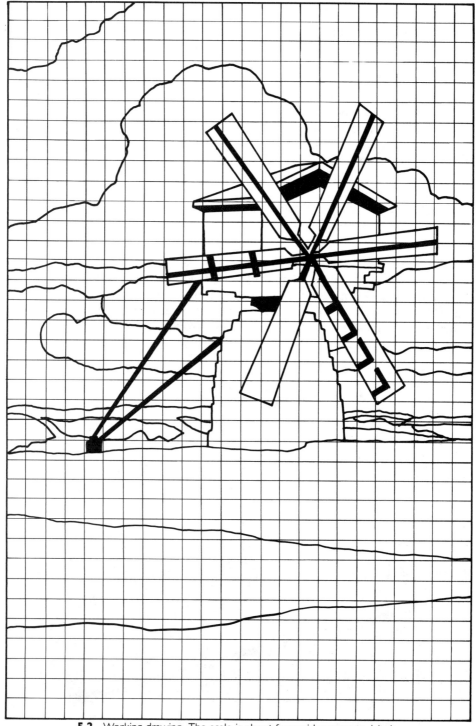

**5-2** Working drawing. The scale is about four grid squares to 1 inch.

## TOOLS AND MATERIALS

In addition to the items listed on p. xi, you need:

- A sheet of waster veneer at about 8 × 12 inches; go for an easy-to-cut veneer type like obeche or sycamore.
- A sheet of backing or compensating veneer; choose an inexpensive type.
- A baseboard at 6 × 9 inches.
- A sheet of tracing paper at about 8 × 12 inches.
- A sheet of carbon paper.
- Several sheets of newspaper.
- A tin of grain sealer.
- A couple of clamping boards.
- Two sheets of plastic.
- The use of clamps or a press.
- A tin of beeswax.

## THE PROJECT

Carefully trace off the design and hinge the tracing edge-to-edge to the waster veneer. Use masking tape for the hinge, and make sure that the design is well placed (FIG. 5-3). Slide a sheet of carbon paper under the tracing and use a hard pencil to press transfer the lines of the design through to the waster veneer, making sure the lines are crisp and clear. Remove the carbon paper and hinge the trac-

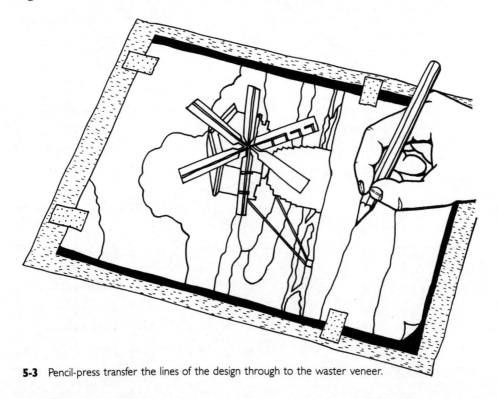

**5-3** Pencil-press transfer the lines of the design through to the waster veneer.

ing back out of the way. Bearing in mind that the waster veneer is going to be left for the sky areas, lightly chalk these areas off on both the tracing and the veneer itself.

When you cut the first window, choose a large feature, such as the big cloud. Then score around the feature with the point of the knife.

When the first window has been carefully marked out, make several passes over the line with the scalpel until the piece is free. Slide your chosen veneer under the waster so that you can see it through the window, and variously turn it this way and that, until you have the grain placed for best effect. Fix the veneer in place with masking tape and use the scalpel to mark in the window outline.

Remove the ''cloud'' veneer and cut away the waste, aiming for a good fit in the window. Press the cut piece into the window and hold it in place with masking tape, placing the tape on the back of the picture.

Continue repeatedly cutting out and filling in windows until you have exchanged most of the waster with choice veneers (FIG. 5-4). When you have what you consider is a finished design, set strips of masking tape over the whole best face of the picture, and peel away all the backing tabs—all the little pieces of tape that were used to hold the individual windows in place.

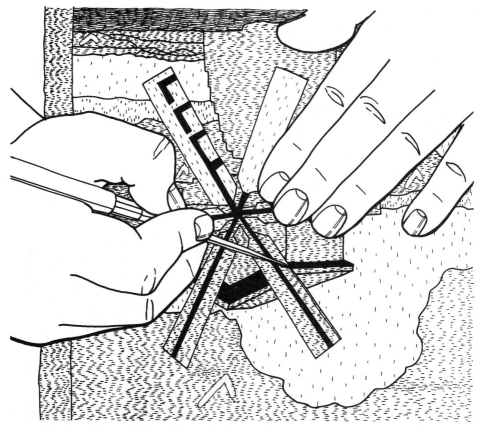

**5-4** Cut out and fit the windows. The chalk ticks mark the waster veneer areas that need to be left.

One piece at a time, smear the white PVA glue over the backing veneer and the picture. The stacking or clamping order is: six sheets of newspaper, a sheet of plastic, the backing veneer, the base board, the marquetry picture, another sheet of plastic and, finally, another six sheets of newspaper (FIG. 5-5, top). Then put the whole sandwich in the press and clamp up (FIG. 5-5, bottom).

When the glue is completely dry, remove the boards, newspaper, and plastic, and peel off the masking tape. Be sure to ease the tape off carefully so that you don't tear up the veneers.

Rub the face of the work down with the graded sandpapers until it is free from bits of glue and newspaper, working back and forth for a smooth finish (FIG. 5-6, top). Once the veneer is both clean and free from dust, give it a coat of sealer.

Rub the marquetry down with the finest glass/garnet paper wrapped around a cork pad. Give the work a generous polish with plain wax and the job is done (FIG. 5-6, bottom).

## HINTS

When you cut the veneers to fit the windows, always cut little by little; never try to slice through the veneer at a single stroke.

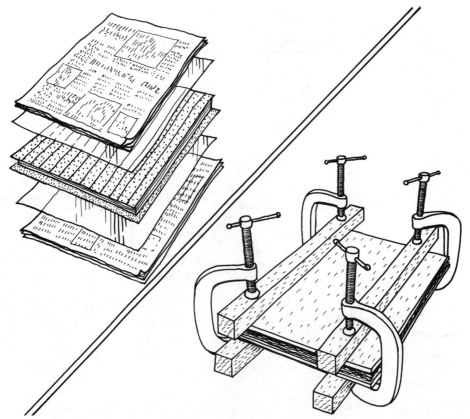

**5-5** Be sure to stack and clamp the pieces in the correct order.

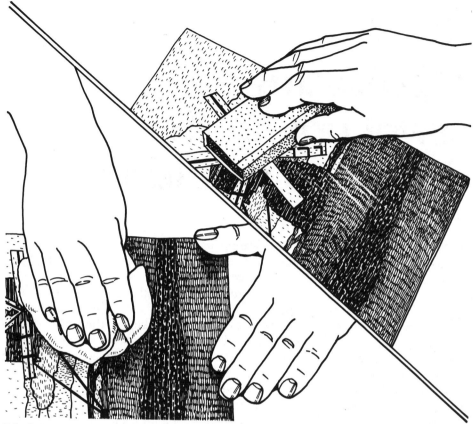

**5-6** Rub the face of the work down with the cork block and the finest garnet paper; don't rub through the veneer thickness or round-over the edges (top). Give the work a generous coat of wax polish with a cotton cloth (bottom).

If you think that a particular feature should have a swift change of grain direction, consider splitting the feature and having two windows.

When you clamp the piece, make sure the various layers are completely free from bits of dust, dirt, and debris. Small fragments of dust caught between layers will ruin a project.

# 6

# Decorating a jewel box in the Sheraton tradition

If you want to make shell, scoop, or scallop marquetry inlay motifs in the classical English furniture tradition, you really need look no further than Sheraton. When most people think of or describe a piece of furniture as being "Sheraton," they think of furniture characterized by lightness, elegance, the extensive use of marquetry, and—perhaps most important of all—the use of various inlay motifs.

You can easily remember the Sheraton style by thinking of the six Ss—Sheraton, shell, scallop, sand, shading, and scorching. All Sheraton marquetry inlay shell and scallop motifs are achieved by the use of the shading technique known as sand-scorching.

If you want to know more about Sheraton, here's your first lead. Thomas Sheraton, 1751–1806, was an English furniture maker and author of the influential *Cabinet-Maker and Upholsterer's Drawing Book* published in 1791.

## CONSIDERING THE PROJECT

Have a good look at the project picture and the working drawing (FIGS. 6-1 and 6-2), and see how the project relates to making and using a traditional sand-scorched and shaded scallop motif, and to covering a plain plywood box with veneer. Note also how the box lid is further decorated with stringers of contrasting, *white wood*, or thin strips of veneer that have been cut, mitered and set frame-like into the mahogany surround.

Focus your attention on the diamond-shaped central motif and see how it is made from four contrasting veneers—a dyed black wood for the outer frame and the central diamond surround, highly grained kingwood for the outer crossbanding, rosewood for the scallop surround, and sycamore for the sand-scorched scalloping and the central scalloped diamond. See how the shaded and scalloped sycamore looks three-dimensional. There are many ways to work a project like this, so if you feel a part needs to be cut and worked before another, simply adjust the order of work accordingly.

**6-1** Project picture. Note the tradition scorched, shaded, and scalloped motif. Note the corner miters.

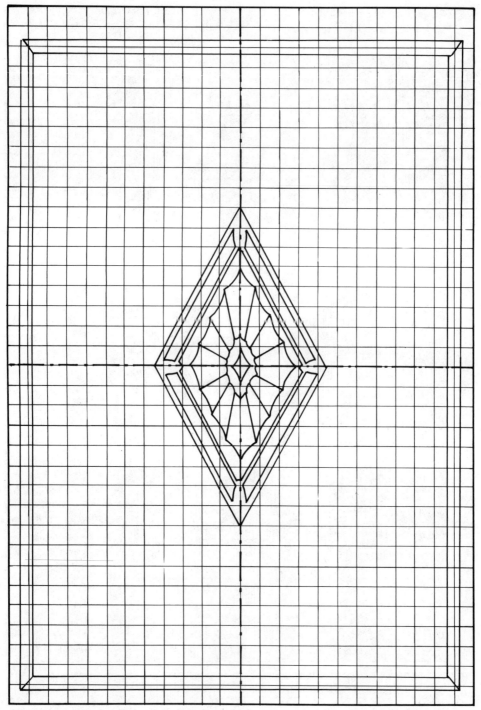

**6-2** Working drawing. The scale is about four grid squares to 1 inch. Note how the central scalloping is made up from fourteen wedge-shaped pieces.

## TOOLS AND MATERIALS

In addition to the items listed on p. xi, you need:

- A white wood box about 6 inches wide, 4 inches deep, and 9 inches long; it's best to buy an inexpensive ready-made plywood box.
- A quantity of mahogany veneer, enough to generously cover the outside base, ends, sides and top.
- A small length of sycamore veneer for the stringers and the shaded motif.
- A sheet of card for the inlay waster.
- A small sheet of dyed black sycamore veneer for the motif.
- A small off-cut of kingwood veneer for the crossbanding.
- A small sheet of rosewood veneer for the inner diamond.
- A pair of scissors.
- An old saucepan or frying pan.
- A small amount of clean silver sand, enough to fill the pan to a depth of about 2 inches.
- The use of a gas or an electric cooker.
- A pair of tweezers/pliers.
- The use of an electric iron.
- A pad of felt or a piece of old carpet.
- A sheet of tracing paper.
- A cotton cloth.
- A tin of wax polish.

## THE PROJECT

Having studied the project picture and the working drawings, trace off the motif design and pencil-press transfer the central scalloping details through to the sheet of white card. Use a pencil and ruler to extend the wedge lines beyond the scallops. With the safety ruler and scalpel, cut out a single wedge window. Slide a sheet of sycamore behind the hole and make sure that the grain runs from end to center (FIG. 6-3, top). Cut the sycamore to fit the window.

Heat the silver sand for about 30 minutes and do a scorching test with a few scraps of veneer. Use the tweezers to slide the veneer into the sand. Each shading will take about five or six seconds. When, by trial and error, you are able to achieve a well-graded and toned effect, then start scorching the wedge-shaped cutout for real (FIG. 6-3, bottom). Aim for a graded scorch that runs about 1/8 inch into the side of each wedge. Note carefully which side of the cutout needs to be scorched.

Continue cutting, scorching and fitting the wedges that will make up the motif. Reassemble the shaded wedges and carefully fit and fix them with masking tape on the glue-face side.

Reestablish the pencil-press transferred lines and use the scalpel to cut the scalloped profiles at side and center. If necessary, reinforce delicate short-grain areas with more tape (FIG. 6-4, top).

Put the shaded and scalloped diamond to one side and take up the black veneer. Establish the shape of the small central scalloped diamond at the center,

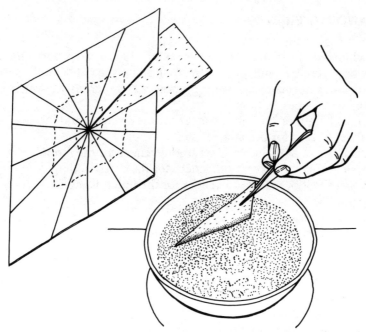

**6-3** Slide the choice veneer under the wedge-shaped window and position it so that the grain runs to the center (top). Use tweezers to slide the wedge-shaped veneer into the hot sand (bottom).

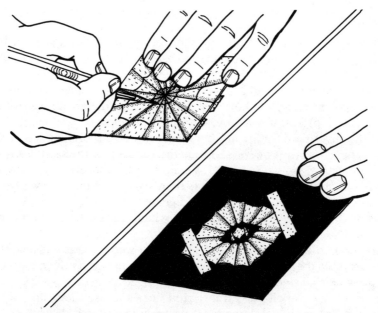

**6-4** Re-establish the lines of the design and cut away the unwanted veneer at center and sides (top). With the white central diamond taped in place, slide the black veneer under the large shaded and scalloped diamond (bottom).

and cut out the first window. Slide a scrap of white sycamore under the diamond window. Mark, cut, trim, and fit the piece, and then hold the cutout in place with tape.

Slide the black veneer under the large shaded and scalloped diamond, and carefully position the motif so that it is centered within the scalloped-edged window. Hold this in place with tape (FIG. 6-4, bottom).

Mark, cut, trim and fit the diamond and black detail. You should now have three elements fitted one within another—the small diamond at the center, the surround of black veneer, and the scalloped and shaded diamond.

Set the large scalloped diamond on the rosewood veneer and mark out the scallop-edged profile. Cut out the window, and fit and tape the diamond within the rosewood veneer. When you have achieved all the little cuts, windows, and infills that make up the center of the motif, take the larger sheet of black veneer and mark and cut the big diamond window, noting the little nicks at the corners. Then slide the central assembly under the window and mark, cut, and fit again.

Continue, marking, cutting and fitting the various windows and cutouts that make up the design. When you come to fitting the narrow crossband strips of kingwood at the outer limits of the motif, make sure you have the grain running in the correct direction (FIG. 6-5, top).

When you have achieved what you consider is a well cut and fitted motif, strap the motif up with tape on the right side, and carefully peel away any tape buildup. Take the large sheet of top-of-box mahogany and cut it to slightly overlap the edges of the box lid. Fix the center by marking out diagonals and quarters, then mark, cut, and fit the assembled motif.

When you come to fitting and fixing the white stringers you should mark, cut, and fit as already described, only this time, cut them longer so that the strips cross at the corners, and cut through the cross-over to make perfect mitered corners (FIG. 6-5, bottom).

Set out all the sheets of covering veneer and check that they are a generous fit. Switch the electric iron on to medium, and cut out the various sheets of thermoplastic gluefilm slightly oversize. Place the film glue-side-down on the box face, and run the hot iron back and forth over the film. Peel away the backing paper, set the veneer best-face-up on the glue-covered box face, and cover the veneer with the backing paper. Run the iron back and forth again over the paper until the glue has melted and the veneer is stuck down. Then remove the backing paper, and use a pad of felt to apply pressure to any loose or bubbled areas of veneer. Be sure to do this before the veneer cools (FIG. 6-6, top).

When you have covered each box face, set the box face down on the clean cutting mat and use the scalpel to carefully trim off the waste veneer. Make sure the blade doesn't run into the grain and splinter the veneer (FIG. 6-6, bottom). If necessary, use the thickness of a metal straight to cut the veneer slightly oversize and then sand back to a flush edge.

First cover the box bottom, then the ends, sides, and top. When you fit the top sheet, make sure the tape-covered side is uppermost.

Finally, remove all the tape, rub the various corner edges and faces down

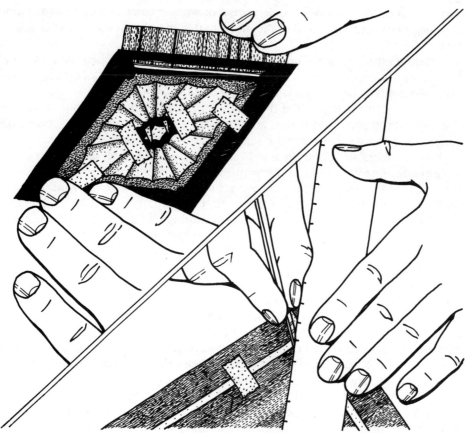

**6-5** When you fit the narrow crossband strips of kingwood at the outer limits of the motif, make sure that the grain is running across the strips (top). Cross the stringers at the corners and achieve the miter by running the knife diagonally through the crossover (bottom).

with the graded garnet papers, and bring the whole workpiece to a wax-burnished finish.

## HINTS

Veneers are easily charred and damaged, so be careful not to over-scorch the wedges. Figure on a scorch time of about four to six seconds.

Use tweezers or pliers to handle the veneer while it is being scorched. Test with a piece of scrap veneer, starting with a 4-second dip, and adjust the time to suit.

If you over-scorch the wedges, they will shrink.

If, when you are ironing the veneer onto the box, it pulls away at the edges, apply pressure to the hot veneer by rubbing with a pad of felt or carpet. Run the pad across the surface and ease it over the edges.

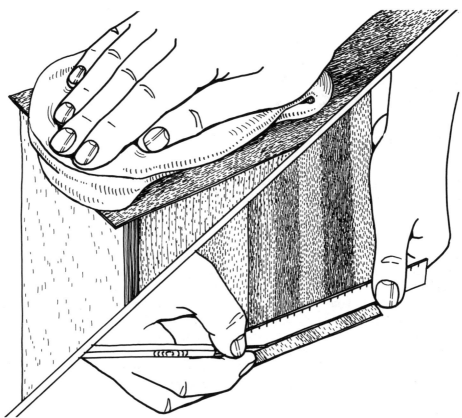

**6-6** Use the pad of felt to apply pressure to the loose or bubbly areas before the veneer cools (top). Use a straightedge and scalpel to carefully trim the edges of waste (bottom).

# 7

# Making & decorating a valet figure

Tutankhamon, a king at 9 and dead at 19 is probably the most famous of all the Egyptian pharaohs. We all know about archaeologist Howard Carter, the sealed tomb, the golden coffins, and the solid gold and bejewelled mask. These are all wonderful, but did you know about the countless inlaid boxes, chests, chairs and coffers also found in the tomb? Well, as you might guess, these boxes and coffers are all ablaze with inlay, but Tutankhamon's ceremonial chair must surely be the most beautiful, the most wonderful, and the most accomplished example of furniture marquetry and inlay in existence. The back and side panels and the seat are literally covered with inlay—line upon line of intricate pattern—thousands of little pieces of colored wood, precious stones, small discs of bright blue ceramic paste, all built into the most breathtakingly beautiful design. Most would agree that ancient Egyptian marquetry and inlay, as made over three thousand years ago in the reign of Tutankhamon, is the best of the best.

When we first saw examples of Egyptian inlay our first thought was, "Wow, how amazing!" And our second thought was, how could we possibly use such eye-dazzling imagery and techniques in our own very humble work? Well, after a great deal of thought we came up with the valet figure idea. Valet figures are decorative, flatwood chairside figures that are designed to stand and hold a tray. We thought it would be a novel idea to combine the valet figure with the imagery and make a pharaoh-type figure all decorated with marquetry and inlay in the Egyptian tradition.

## CONSIDERING THE PROJECT

Have a look at the project picture and the working drawing to see how, at a scale of one grid square to 1 inch, the figure stands about 36 inches high and about 15–18 inches wide (FIGS. 7-1, and 7-2). Note the easy-to-make slot-fixing of the tray and base, and see how the Egyptian inlay technique is used to good effect to decorate the various borders, patterns, and motifs that make up the design. Note how the broad, flat areas of face, chest, arms, and legs are worked using the window technique, and how between the legs and arm/body parts, the white ground

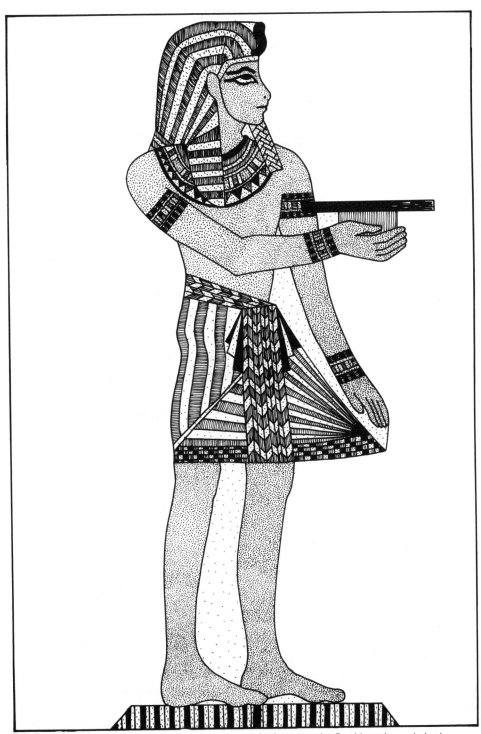

**7-1** Project picture. Note how the tray and the base are slot-fixed into the main body.

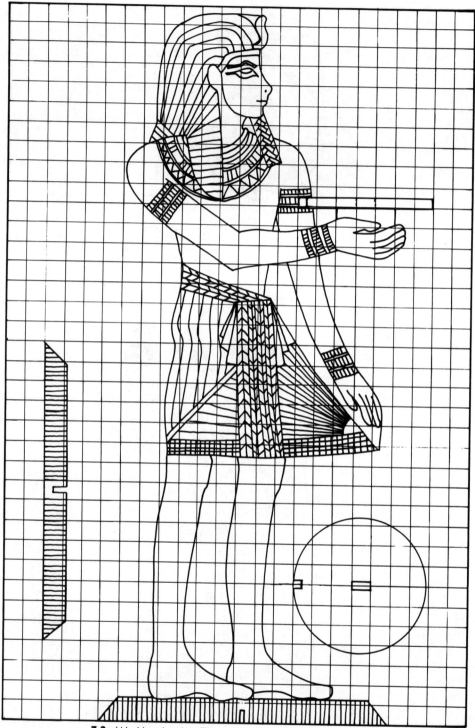

**7-2** Working drawing. The scale is one grid square to 1 inch.

sycamore is left untouched. The only tricky areas are the design lines that have to be left as positive gaps and topped up with black filler—the jaw line, the lips, the fingers, etc.

Finally, note how the figure is cut from best quality 1/2-inch-thick, birch-faced, multicore plywood, and see also how the cut edge has been rubbed down and stained.

One of the best things about working a project of this nature is that there is plenty of room for your own whims and fancies. If you want to change the design, have more inlay, make a pair of figures, use a mixture of painting, marquetry, and inlay, add brass and silver inlay, then no problem—the brief is wide open.

## TOOLS AND MATERIALS

In addition to the items listed on p. xi, you need:
- A sheet of best quality 1/2-inch-thick multicore plywood at about 24 × 36 inches.
- A good quantity of pink-brown veneer for the flesh tones; use an attractive, easy-to-work wood like peartree.
- A good quantity of white sycamore for the background/waster, enough for each side of the figure.
- A good selection of dyed wood for the ceremonial wig and beard and for all the costume trim and decoration; use bright, sharp colors to include: turquoise blue, gray-blue, red, yellow, brown, orange, white, and black.
- A large sheet of tracing paper.
- A couple of square yards of gluefilm.
- A tin of black filler.
- A pair of long-nose tweezers/forceps.
- A coping/fret saw, or the use of a power jigsaw.
- A hand drill with a needle drill bit.
- An electric flat iron.
- A pair of scissors.
- A black felt tip marker—with turps/alcohol ink.
- A tin of polyurethane varnish.

## THE PROJECT

At a scale of one grid square to 1 inch, the figure stands about 36 inches high and 18 inches wide. Trace off the design, cut the tracing into six sections, and then use a photocopy machine to blow the design up to size.

Use a ruler, knife, and masking tape to build two large ground/waster sheets with the white sycamore, each at 20 × 36 inches. This allows for waste. Tape the six photocopy enlargements together and trace the design off onto a single large sheet of tracing paper. Pencil-press transfer the lines of the traced design through to the two sheets of white sycamore veneer. Make sure you have two identical but mirror-imaged figures—one for each side of the valet figure (FIG. 7-3, left).

Repeat the procedure, only this time, pencil-press transfer the lines of the traced figure, tray, and stand through to the sheet of plywood. Use your coping/

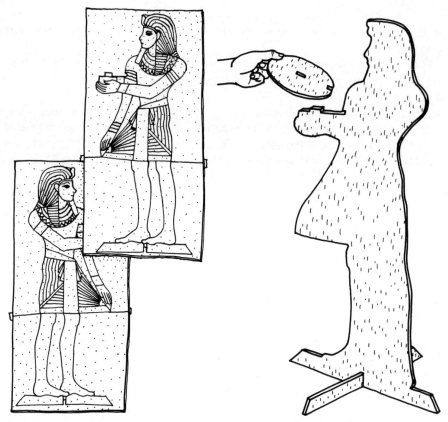

**7-3** Pencil-press transfer the lines of the traced design through to the sheets of the white sycamore veneer (left). Have a trial fitting of the plywood figure to make sure that the slot fixings are a good tight fit (right).

fret/power saw to cut out the plywood profile, the figure, the tray, and the stand. Pay particular attention to the face details. Have a trial fitting, and use the graded sandpaper to bring it to good order. Aim to rub the cut edges down so that they are crisp and square and the slot fixings are a good, tight fit (FIG. 7-3, right).

Having cut out the plywood forms and transferred the design through to both sheets of white sycamore, take one of the veneer sheets and remount and hinge the tracing at the top edge. Now, starting with the shape that makes up the face, use the scalpel to cut out the first window (FIG. 7-4, top).

Slide a sheet of peartree veneer behind the hole, move it around for best grain effect, and use the point of the scalpel to mark through the window outline. Remove the peartree veneer to the cutting mat and cut out the shape. In this instance, aim for a slightly loose fit around the jaw and browline and a perfect fit along the outside figure profile line.

Fit the cutout into the window and fix it at the back with masking tape. Flip the tracing over and redraw the features onto the pearwood. With the tracing hinged back out of the way, establish the mouth shape by cutting a slot with the

**7-4** Cut out the face window from the white sycamore veneer; be careful when you come to the jawline (top). Fit the pearwood veneer so that there is a positive filler gap; tape at the back of the wood (bottom).

scalpel. Try to stay with a delicate line. The mouth, the nostril, the lines between the fingers, and so on will all become visible when they are filled (FIG. 7-4, bottom).

Continue cutting and fitting all the windows that make up the face, chest, arms, and legs. Note carefully the joints that need to be filled, especially the face details and the hands.

When you have window-cut and fitted all the skin areas, cut out the whole window shape of the wrist bangle/band. Use the scalpel and safety ruler to cut out on your chosen colored veneer all the little mosaic strips and tiles that make the band design. (NOTE: You might use a parquetry jig; see other projects.)

Set out two to four strips of masking tape and arrange them side by side, sticky-side-up. Fix them to the work surface with strips of tape. Now, set about the tricky task of arranging the various mosaic pieces. Use your fingertips, the point of the scalpel, and the tweezers to place them side-by-side and best-side-up on the sticky tape surface (FIG. 7-5, top).

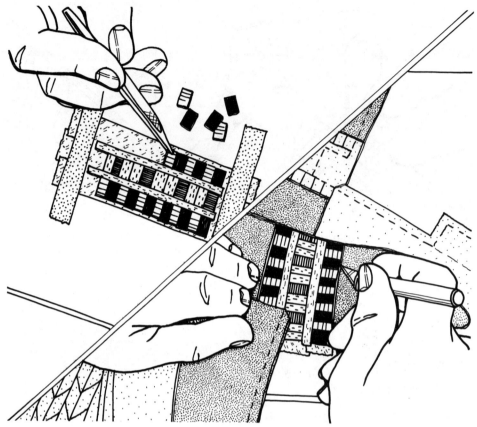

**7-5** Use the tweezers to place the mosaic pieces onto the sticky tape (top). Slide the made-up mosaic under the wrist window and carefully mark through the hole with the point of the scalpel (bottom).

Continue carefully positioning a single veneer shape on the sticky tape at a time until the design is complete. Make sure that you allow for generous adjustment and trim wastage.

Having built-up the sheet of mosaic inlay, slide it under the wrist window and mark, cut, fit, and fix it, just as you might a straightforward sheet of choice veneer (FIG. 7-5, bottom).

Fit the first wrist band, then continue in the same manner, building and fitting the other wrist band, the two upper arm bands, the strip of pattern along the base, the sash, the collar and so on. Work back and forth across the design, cutting windows and building mosaics to fit.

When you come to fitting the wig strips, use the window technique as described. This time, however, crossband the veneer grain by having the grain run across the width of the strips. You will, of course, need to cut and fit various pieces of veneer together in much the same way as when you built the mosaics.

When you consider the design finished—when the various design windows that make up the design have been either replaced with choice veneers or with made up mosaics, or simply left as areas of white sycamore—then set strips of masking tape out over the best face of the assembly. Carefully peel off all the tabs of masking tape from the back and cut the figure away from its background, leaving a 1/8-inch overlap at the outer edges. Do this with both figures.

Next, cover the tray with veneer, complete the stand marquetry (FIG. 7-6, top), and spend some time placing and trimming all the marquetry assemblies to a good fit. Set them on the plywood cutout and trim the veneer and/or the plywood, until you consider it finished. Then, completing one side of the valet figure at a time, set about fitting and fixing the veneer assemblies.

Position the gluefilm paper-side-up on the plywood, allowing for a generous overlap, and tack it at side and center with the hot iron. Peel the backing paper away from the gluefilm, being careful not to pull away any areas of glue. Set the assembly carefully in position, making sure that it is perfectly aligned, and spread the backing paper over the heat-sensitive veneers. Work the hot iron back and forth from center to side, until all the glue has melted. If there are any bubbles or air pockets, reheat them and apply pressure with felt or carpet, pressing down

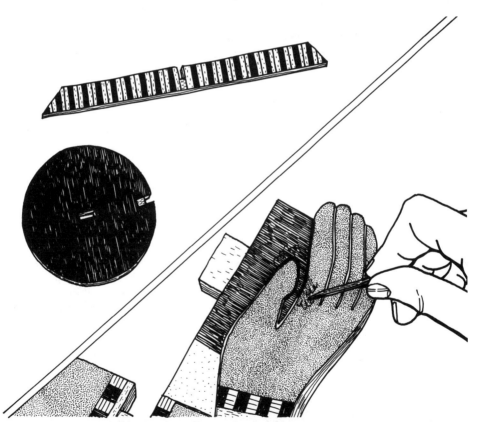

**7-6** Make sure that you leave the slot-fixing areas on the tray and the stand unveneered (top). Work the black filler into all the joints, especially the design details between the finger joints (bottom).

firmly until the glue has cooled. Trim back all edges with the scalpel, and repeat the procedure on the other side of the plywood cutout.

Seal all faces and edges, wait for the sealer to dry, and work the black filler into all joints. Pay particular attention to the joints that define the face, the jaw, the mouth line, the line around the ears and throat, between the fingers, etc. (FIG. 7-6, bottom).

Use the felt-tip marker to black all the plywood edges. Work around the profile, following the contours. Be careful that the ink does not bleed into the grain.

Finally, using a block and graded papers, rub the whole workpiece down to a smooth finish, lay on a couple of coats of polyurethane varnish, and the job is done.

## HINTS

If you can't get to a photocopy machine, use graph paper to enlarge the design.

Best start out this project by finding a color photograph showing Egyptian imagery. Or, better still, visit a large city museum and see a mummy or a mural.

Many of the joints between windows also define form and shape, and are going to be topped up with a black filler. For this reason, these joints need to be loose-fitting; aim for a 1/16- to 1/8-inch gap.

You might change the design and use ready-made bandings to create the design areas. The problem with this is that bandings tend to be thicker than veneers, so you will have to spend more time at the sanding stage.

# 8

# Decorating a mirror in art deco style

**R**ussian ballet and cubism, fast cars and airplanes, trains and cinema, archaeological finds in Egypt and Central America, and jazz—art deco has been described as: . . .

"Those tremendous years between the wars . . . 1919–1938 . . . It was a time for Bright Young People—women's hair was at its shortest, hats were bell-shaped and cloche, lips were cupid's bows, and jazz and the Charleston were all the rage."

It's not easy to define art deco because, after all, it was made up of many different styles. That said, the art and craft objects of the period are characterized by being bold, brightly colored, formalized, and geometric. No more pretty flowers and soft delicate tendrils but rather a great many sunbursts, zigzags, lightning motifs, ziggurats, and machine-inspired geometry.

Of course, the furniture and woodwares went along with the feel of the times. No more looking back towards eighteenth century marquetry and nineteenth century art and craft oak. Art deco furniture of the 1920s was squarish, stepped, and, above all, encrusted with marquetry and inlay. The designers favored the use of rare woods like amaranthe, macassar ebony, and violet wood. They liked contrasts—black woods and chrome, mother of pearl and inlaid brass—all beautiful!

## CONSIDERING THE PROJECT

Have a look at the project picture and the two working drawings (FIGS. 8-1 and 8-2), and see how, at a grid scale of four squares to 1 inch, the mirror measures 6 × 9 inches. Note how the base is made up from three thicknesses of thin plywood, with the small mirror tile being sandwiched and framed between the layers. Note that the project uses three materials—stained black veneer, yellow white boxwood veneer, and a delicate arrowhead inlay banding. As you can see, the veneers and the arrowhead banding are laid up in alternating strips and then knife-cut on a jig to make a stripped 60/30° ribbon-like parquetry material.

**8-1** Project picture. See how the project uses stained black sycamore, yellow boxwood, and delicate arrowhead banding.

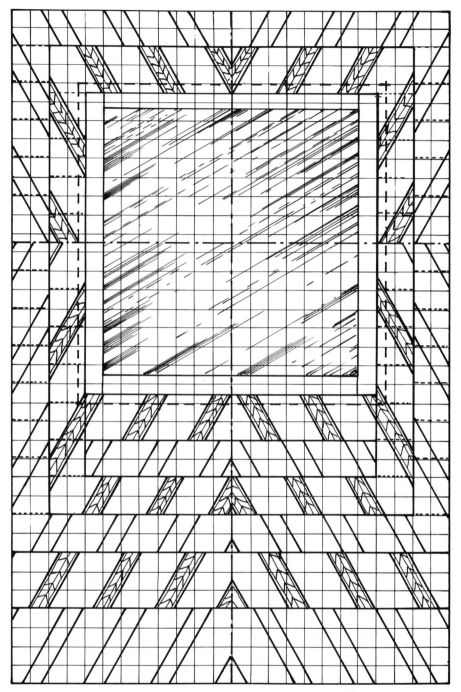

**8-2** Working drawing. The scale is about four grid squares to 1 inch. Note the various ribbon width changes.

Run a ruler over the working drawing and see how the main total design is made up from three ribbon widths—$1/2$ inch, $5/8$ inch, and $3/4$ inch. Of course, if you like the project but want to go for a more basic design, there's no reason why you shouldn't adjust and simplify the design to suit. You could, for example, modify the design to a single ribbon width, or you could make all the ribbons of black veneer and inlay banding rather than introduce the narrow strips of boxwood. Study the design, taking all the implications of the project into account and then adjust the design accordingly.

## TOOLS AND MATERIALS

In addition to the items listed on p. xi, you need:

- Three pieces of $1/8$- to $3/16$-inch-thick plywood at $6 \times 9$ inches.
- A sheet of dyed black sycamore at $6 \times 18$ inches.
- A sheet of boxwood veneer at about $6 \times 9$ inches.
- A small sheet of peartree veneer for the small inner frame.
- A small mirror tile at about $4^{1}/4 \times 4^{1}/4$ inches, no more than $1/8$ inch thick.
- The use of a workbench with a vice or a clamp.
- A small hand drill with a $1/16$-inch drill bit.
- A coping type saw with a pack of spare blades.
- A couple of yards of banding; go for the three-color arrowhead pattern at about $1/4$ inch wide.
- A sheet of thermoplastic gluefilm at about $7 \times 10$ inches.
- A good supply of workout paper.
- A sheet of tracing paper.
- A 30/60° metal or plastic set square.
- A metal straightedge.
- A small amount of wood filler.
- A tin of wax polish.
- The use of an electric flat iron.
- A quantity of old clean fluff-free cotton sheeting.

## THE PROJECT

Have a look at the project picture, the working drawings and the cutting grid (FIGS. 8-1, 8-2, and 8-3). See how the design fits together. Note the various ribbon sizes and the way the design is quartered. When you have a good understanding of the project, take the three prepared $1/8$-inch-thick $6 \times 9$ inch plywood boards and label them "A," "B," and "C." Use a pencil, square, and ruler to set out the position of the mirror tile. Draw out board "A" so that the $3^{1}/2$-inch-square hole is set in $1^{1}/4$ inches from the top and the side. Draw out board "B" so that the $4^{1}/4$-inch-square hole is set in from the top by 1 inch and the sides by $7/8$ inch.

With the mirror holes well placed, use a drill and coping saw to clear away the waste, then make a trial dry fitting. If all is well, the three boards should fit together so that the mirror tile is nicely sandwiched and contained, and the top hole is slightly smaller all round than the mirror (FIG. 8-4, top).

Put boards "B" and "C" to one side and trace off the working drawing (FIG.

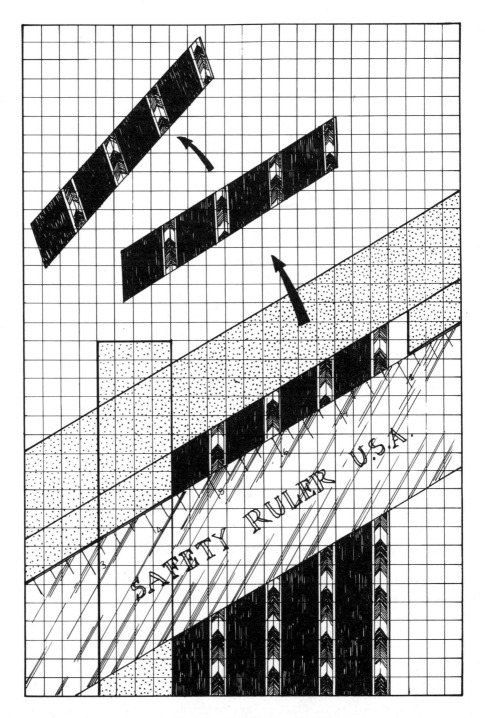

**8-3** Cutting jig/grid. The scale is four grid squares to 1 inch. Note that you will have to modify the jig to suit the various ribbon/strip widths.

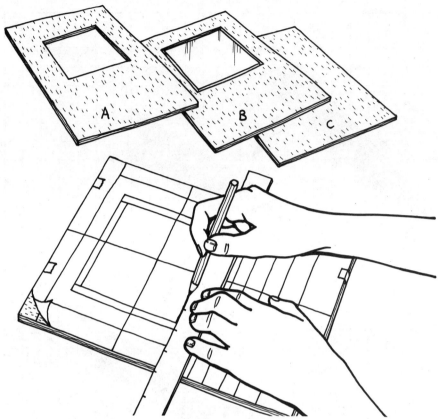

**8-4** Cut the plywood and have a trial fitting (top). Pencil-press transfer the design through to board "A" (bottom).

8-2). Pencil-press transfer the lines of the design through to board "A," the top board (FIG. 8-4, bottom).

Now take the cutting mat, the 60/30° set square, and the masking tape and set out the 60° cutting jig. Have a 1/2-inch-wide veneer channel and double check all angles. Cut the 18-inch-long piece of dyed black sycamore into two pieces at 9 inches each. Use the jig to cut the sheets into 1/2-inch-wide strips. You should end up with twenty-four 9-inch-long, 1/2-inch-wide strips.

Cut the arrowhead banding into 9-inch lengths. Place two strips of tape sticky-side-up on the work surface. Place four strips each of arrowhead and black onto the tape; they should alternate black/arrowhead/black/arrowhead, etc. Then press the strips so that they are held firmly together (FIG. 8-5, top) and tape the strips together.

Next slide the eight-strip panel into the jig and cut off a couple of angled 1/2-inch-wide ribbons with the craft knife (FIG. 8-3). Adjust the jig and cut strips at 5/8 inch wide and 3/4 inch—no more than two strips of each. When you have a supply of black and arrowhead ribbons, repeat the procedure, only this time alternate the black veneer and narrow strips of boxwood.

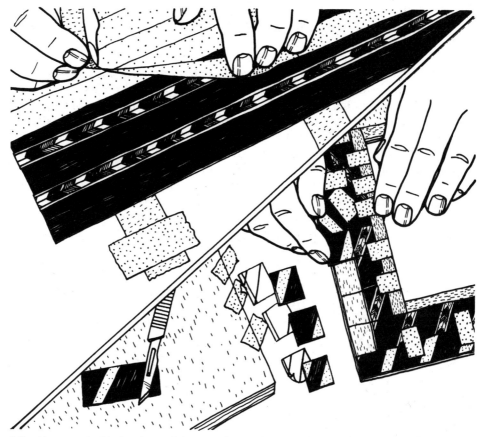

**8-5** Alternate the black strips and the arrowhead banding and tape them together (top). As each part is fitted, fix it to its neighbor with a small tab of masking tape (bottom).

With the top board and the tracing, cut and fit all the little pieces that will make up the design. Search out the pieces of best fit by cutting the tracing down into best-fit pattern pieces. As each strip or part strip is fitted, fix it to its neighbor with masking tape (FIG. 8-5). NOTE: Make sure there is a very slight overlap around the outer edge of the board.

Remember, the total design is split, quartered, and symmetrical. Therefore, when you come to fitting the top left and the bottom right quarters, you have to adjust the veneer ribbons so that the masking tape is on the other side and all the arrowheads angle in and look towards the mirror.

Continue working little by little, until the design is complete, and until the best face of the panel is almost completely covered with masking tape. Note how the areas on each side of the mirror are made from many small sections.

When you have what you consider a well-fitted design, set the sheet of glu-film glue-side-down over the top plywood board and smooth over the surface with the hot iron. Don't worry too much at this stage about melting all the film; just make sure that it is tacked here and there.

When the film has cooled, peel away the backing paper and carefully set the veneer panel tape-side-up on the gluefilm. Fiddle and fit until the veneer is correctly placed.

With the tape-covered surface now face up, cover the veneer with the sheeting and the backing paper and swiftly work the hot iron back and forth until the glue has melted (FIG. 8-6, top). Wait for the glue to cool, and then very carefully peel away all the masking tape, one piece at a time, until the best face of the design is completely clear of tape. Use a spirit-dampened cloth to remove all traces of the masking tape, and trim all veneer edges to a good finish.

Now use the white PVA glue to fit and fix the three plywood boards that make up the mirror. Smear glue on the base sheet and set the middle sheet and the mirror tile in position. Smear glue on the middle sheet and set the top veneer decorated sheet in place. Make sure all three sheets are aligned, then put them under pressure between sheets of paper until the glue has gone off (FIG. 8-6, bottom). Use the graded garnet paper to rub the work down to a smooth finish, and stain the

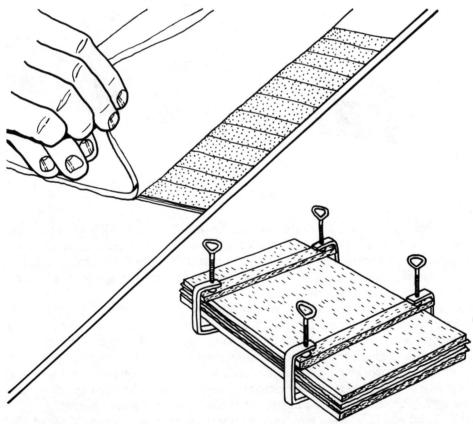

**8-6** Pad and protect the veneer assembly by covering it with several layers of old sheeting and with backing paper (top). Make sure the layers are well aligned and then put the whole sandwich in the press until the glue has set (bottom).

edges of the board black. Finally lay on several coats of wax polish, and burnish to a high shine.

## HINTS

When you cut across the arrowhead bands, take several strokes, and be careful that the knife doesn't slip.

When you assemble the small pieces of veneer, have a few tabs of sticky tape ready.

If, when you are putting the pieces together, you find that the masking tape buildup is a bit thick, peel it off and replace it with a larger single thickness.

Traditionalists do not recommend the use of gluefilm with marquetry assemblies, but you won't have problems as long as you work swiftly and surely.

If you need to use the hot iron to realign one or two veneer pieces after peeling off the tape, make sure that you protect the piece with the sheeting and the backing paper.

The arrowhead inlay banding is thicker than the black veneer, so use a block-supported glass paper to reduce the wood thickness.

# 9

# Making a tabletop marquetry motif

**B**oulle describes a type of furniture marquetry that was very popular in France in the seventeenth, eighteenth, and nineteenth centuries. The technique was named after Charles Andre Boulle (1642–1732), a French marquetarian under King Louis XIV. Now known as *boulle, boule,* or even *buhl*, the technique is characterized by its economical use of time and materials—so much so, that boulle marquetry might almost better be described as "two for the price of one."

The main feature of the boulle technique is the layering or sandwiching of sheets of contrasting materials—such as brass, multi-colored veneers, and tortoiseshell—and the cutting through these layers to create a number of identical forms. Once the multi-material stack has been sawn, the various identical cutouts are swapped around and reset.

In the simplest terms, if you take a square sheet of mahogany and a square sheet of sycamore and sandwich them together, cut a circular window through both sheets, and swap the circular cutouts, you end up with a sycamore square with a mahogany inset circle, and a mahogany square with a sycamore inset circle. See what I mean when I say economical? Of course, when half a dozen or so sheets of brass, veneer, and silver are layered and variously intricately pierced and fretted, and the cutouts swapped around and relocated so that motifs are made up of three or more different materials, then the technique becomes really exciting.

If you are looking for a marquetry technique that uses every last scrap of veneer, a technique that is both exciting and challenging, then this is the project for you.

## CONSIDERING THE DESIGN

Have a good long look at the working drawings (FIGS. 9-1 and 9-2) and the how-to stages to see how this piece of boulle work has been quartered and worked from two contrasting veneers. It's best to have one dark veneer and one light veneer. You need four sheets in all, two sheets of each.

See how the cutouts from the four sheets have been swapped around to make a traditional counterbalanced design motif. Note also how the four sheets need to be sandwiched between two waster veneers. As you can see, this project concentrates not so much on the tabletop itself but rather on the stages of cutting and working a boulle design.

**9-1** Project picture. Note that the design has been quartered and the various cutouts counterchanged.

**9-2** Working drawing. The scale is four grid squares to I inch.

Finally, note the direction of the grain and see how, at a grid scale of four squares to 1 inch, the design relates to a quartered 6 × 6 inch square.

## TOOLS AND MATERIALS

In addition to the items listed on p. xi, you need:
- Six sheets of veneer at about 5 × 5 inches—two easy-to-cut waster sheets, two dark mahogany, two light contrasting sycamore.
- A sheet of white workout paper.
- A small amount of black waterproof ink.
- A sheet of tracing paper.
- A sheet of gluefilm.
- A sheet of strong, fine paper; we use mulberry paper tissue.
- A small amount of water-based paste.
- A few drops of vegetable oil.
- A handful of fine stainless-steel veneer pins.
- A tin of grain sealer.
- Wax polish.
- A small table to decorate, plus the surround veneer.
- A small hand drill with a fine-needle drill bit.
- The use of an electric iron.
- A fretsaw/coping saw with a pack of jeweler's piercing blades.

## THE PROJECT

Start by sandwiching the four choice veneers between the two wasters. Make sure the grain on all the sheets runs in the same direction (FIG. 9-3, top). Strap the whole six-sheet stack with masking tape so that all the sheets are stable and well contained. Use the black waterproof ink and the fine mulberry paper to trace off the design, making sure that the lines are crisp and clear.

Give the tissue paper tracing a generous coat of paste. Wait a few moments for the paper to stretch, and then smooth the tracing onto the topmost veneer of the taped sandwich. When the paste is completely dry, rub a few drops of oil into the paper until it becomes semitransparent and the ink lines can be seen; then tap a few stainless steel veneer pins through the stack and around the design (FIG. 9-3, bottom).

Set the stack of veneers on a cutting table or in the vice and carefully saw out the various shapes that make up the design (FIG. 9-4). When you work the small enclosed detail, drill a pilot hole on the cutting line and pass the saw through the hole.

Once you have sawn out all the forms, cut away the waste margins, and use a scalpel to ease the veneer layers apart, grouping the layers according to color and shape. Look again at the master design and have a trial dry fitting.

If all is well, put the whole design together by butt-jointing each piece to its neighbor. Identify a piece, set it facedown alongside a neighboring piece, and then fix it with a tab of masking tape (FIG. 9-5). Continue identifying, locating, trimming to size, and tab-fixing until the whole design is complete.

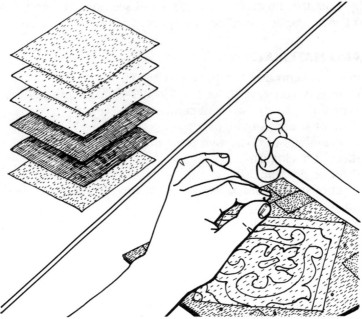

**9-3** Sandwich the four choice veneers between two wasters so that you have a six-sheet stack (top). Tap a few stainless steel veneer pins through and around the design (bottom).

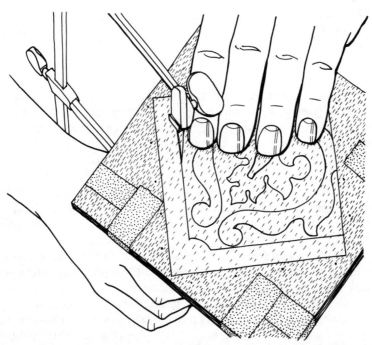

**9-4** Hold the stack firmly down on the cutting table and saw out the various shapes.

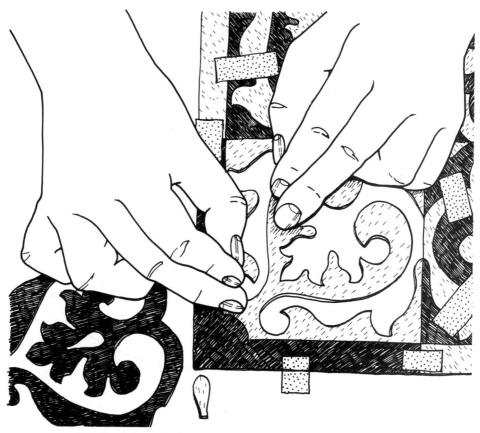

**9-5** Butt-joint each piece to its neighbor and fix it with masking tape.

Remember that each piece of marquetry infill has two possible placings, so try each in turn, and settle for the best fit. Then work through all the windows and counterchanges until the design is complete.

When you have what you consider is a well-set design, set the tabletop to decorate best-face-up on the work surface, and brush out the motif recess. Make sure that all the cracks and corners are completely free of dust and debris. Cut the gluefilm to fit, and set it paper-side-up in the recess.

Smooth the hot iron over the paper surface, just touching it here and there so the glue is tacked down. Wait a few moments for the film to cool and then carefully ease away the paper backing sheet (FIG. 9-6, top). Lay the boulle motif best-face-up in the film-covered recess, place the backing sheet on top of the veneer to protect it from scorching, and work the hot iron back and forth over the surface to melt the glue (FIG. 9-6, bottom). Wait for the glue to cool, then peel off the backing paper and remove the tabs of masking tape, using a small amount of spirit to remove masking tape residue.

Brush on a coat of sealer, and use the garnet paper to rub down the face of the motif. Work through the graded papers until the wood feels completely smooth to

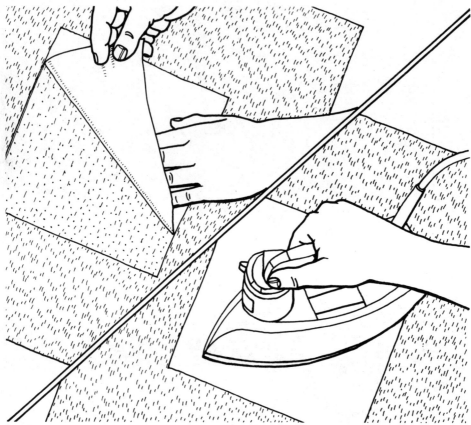

**9-6** Carefully peel the backing paper away from the gluefilm (top). Cover the veneer assembly with the backing paper and melt the glue with a hot iron (bottom).

the touch. Wipe the work down with a spirit-dampened cloth, reseal, wait for the sealer to dry, and give the face a last cutting down with the finest paper.

Finally, use the plain wax polish and a fluff-free cotton cloth to bring the wood to a smooth, burnished finish.

## HINTS

Although the emphasis with this project is on cutting and fitting the boulle motif, you will also have to cut, fit, and glue the large piece of around-the-motif veneer. Use the window method to achieve a perfect fit, and the gluefilm for easy fixing.

If you like the idea of the boulle method but would prefer to decorate a tray, a door, or whatever, simply adjust the stages accordingly.

Make sure that the gluefilm and the work are completely free from dust and debris. To this end, have a good clean up just prior to gluing.

You can sprinkle a few drops of water onto the face of the veneer before ironing; this compensates for an over-hot iron, and for water lost through drying out.

This inlay and parquetry vanity mirror is an excellent example of the art deco style.

The checkers/chess side of this two-sided games board displays the strip parquetry method.

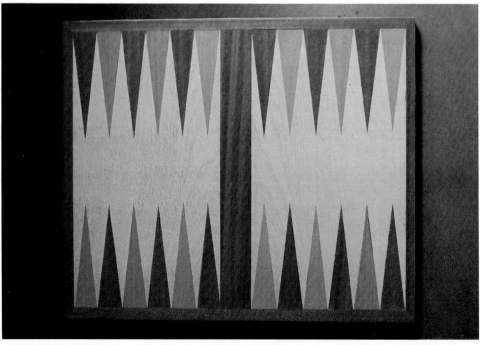

The backgammon side of the games board is created using the window method.

Little diamond shapes of different veneers make up this traditional cube design parquetry table mat.

This beautiful jewel box is sand-scorched and shaded in the Sheraton tradition.

This delightful jigsaw puzzle was created using fretwork and colored veneers.

This marquetry mirror-image tray shows off the fretsawn boulle technique.

# 10
# Making &
# decorating bookends

**F**ifty or so years ago, just about every schoolboy, hobbyist, woodworker and aspiring marquetarian wanted to make and decorate a set of bookends or a book-rack. There were bookracks with wonderfully fixed and fretted uprights and bookends with curiously hinged and pivoted backs; there were bookends with interlocking parts, and dangerously efficient revolving bookracks. There were even bookends that looked like miniature Aztec stepped pyramids. It seems that from about the 1920s right through to the early 1950s, the whole of England, Europe, and America must have been involved in some sort of bookend mania.

OK, so I'm only kidding. But the plain fact is, bookends do pose rather an exciting design problem. The bracket-like L shape, the size, and the structure are all more or less fixed, so you can see that this rather restrictive design and function brief makes for a challenging woodwork project.

As always with a project of this character, there are many points to consider—how to make the form exciting, how to improve upon existing designs, and so on. Of course, all the weird and wonderful fretted, hinged, and pivotted designs are one answer, but in the context of this book at least, we feel that it's best to go for a simple, three-block structure and a marquetry motif that further extends this form. Because the form is already rather monolithic, buttressed, and architectural, we decided to extend the notion, and go for an equally strong architectural motif. And, because the pair of bookends do look rather pyramidical, so we decided to draw our inspiration from an ancient Egyptian painted lotus motif.

## CONSIDERING THE PROJECT

Have a good look at the project picture and the working drawing (FIGS. 10-1 and 10-2), and see how, at a scale of four grid squares to 1 inch, the bookends stand about 5 inches high, 5 inches long, and 3 inches wide. Note the use of prepared 3-inch-wide and 1-inch-thick pine, the simple glued and screwed structure, the way all surfaces are veneered, and the way the inlaid marquetry motif is set in both sides of the bracket angle. You need to make four motifs in all, two for each bookend.

Because of the need for strong contrasts, we have worked the design in three veneer types—dyed black for all faces of the L bracket and for details within the

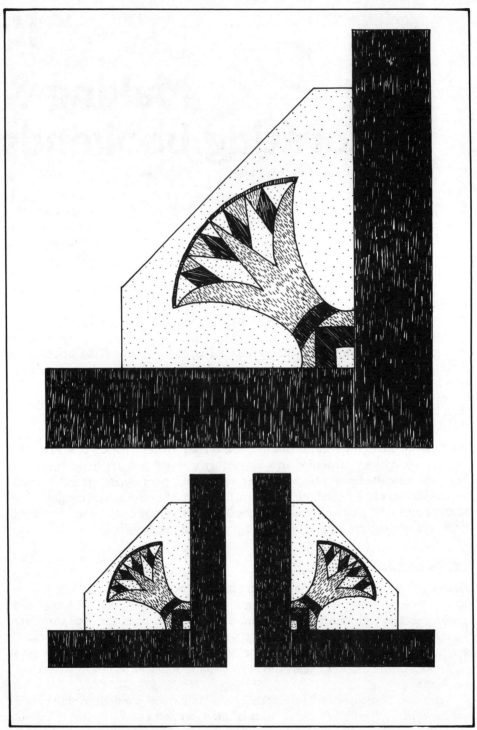

**10-1** Project picture. Note the simple, easy-to-make structure and the bold inlaid motif.

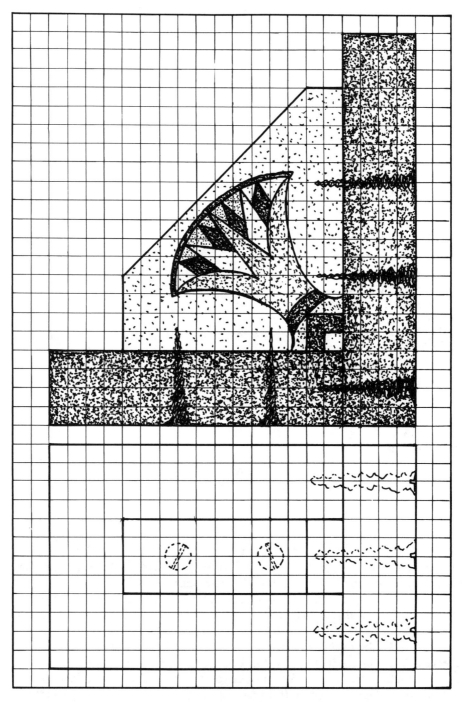

**10-2** Working drawing, (front view and plan). The scale is four grid squares to 1 inch. Note the simple screw fixing.

motif, cream-white box for the angle and some areas within the motif, and silver-gray harewood for other details.

## TOOLS AND MATERIALS

In addition to the items listed on p. xi, you need:
- A piece of 3-inch-wide, 1-inch-thick prepared white pine at about 30 inches long.
- A piece of dyed black sycamore veneer at 10 inches wide and 24 inches long.
- A sheet of white aspen veneer at 10 inches wide and 12 inches long.
- A sheet of silver-gray harewood at about 10 × 10 inches.
- A 36-×-36-inch sheet of gluefilm.
- A sheet each of carbon and tracing paper.
- An electric iron.
- A pad of felt.
- A workbench with a vice.
- A benchhook.
- A set square.
- A short tenon saw.
- A hammer.
- Twelve 1½-inch-long brass screws. Go for thin screws with countersunk heads.
- A screwdriver to fit the screws.
- A hand drill with drill bits to fit the screws.
- A small amount of filler for the countersunk holes.
- A small tin of polyurethane varnish.

## THE PROJECT

Have a look at the project picture and working drawing details (FIGS. 10-1 and 10-2) and see how the two brackets can be cut and worked from the single 30-inch length of 3-inch-wide, 1-inch-thick prepared pine. Use a pencil, ruler, and square to mark the wood accordingly; you need two lengths at 5¼ inches, one at 5 inches, and two at 4 inches. Allow extra wood for wastage.

Carefully measure, mark, and cut down the 5-inch length so that you have two identical, angled bracket/triangle shapes (FIG. 10-3, top). Make sure that all faces, edges, and angles are crisp, true, and square.

Working one bookend at a time, have a trial fitting. Pencil mark the required direction of the grain, and label the bottom and back faces of the main L-shaped bracket (FIG. 10-3, bottom).

Now take the two pieces of wood that make up the L-shaped form, and cut pieces of gluefilm to fit all faces; don't bother at this stage with the back and the bottom. Switch the electric iron on to medium setting and set the main back slab flat down on the workbench, front-face up. Position the gluefilm glue-side-down on the front face, and rub it over with the hot iron (FIG. 10-4, top).

When the film has been tacked in place, carefully peel off the backing paper

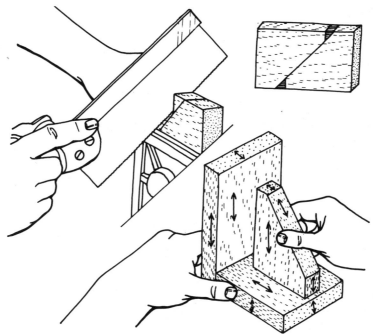

**10-3** Take the 5-inch length and carefully measure, mark, and cut the two angled bracket shapes (top). Have a trial fitting; mark in the direction of the veneer grain (bottom).

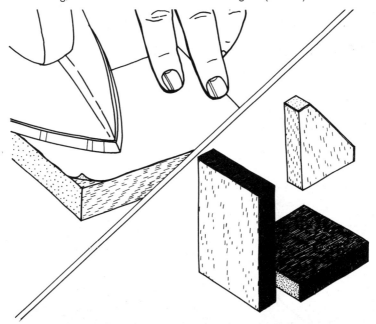

**10-4** Position the gluefilm on the front face and tack it into position with the hot iron (top). At the pre-screwing stage, cover the various faces with veneer, leave the bottom and the back of the main upright and the bottom and mating end of the base uncovered. Also leave the four motif faces of the two angled brackets uncovered (bottom).

and set the sheet of black veneer squarely down on the film-covered surface and cover the veneer with the backing paper. Work it back and forth with the iron.

With the veneer well fitted and fixed, set the workpiece veneer-side-down on the cutting mat and use the scalpel to trim off the waste. Continue covering the various faces and edges with selected veneers.

When you have covered all but the bottom and end of the 4-inch-long base slab and the back of the 5¼-inch endpiece with the black veneer, cover the angled bracket in a like manner, only this time, use the white veneer and only cover the top edges (FIG. 10-4, bottom).

Pencil-press transfer the lotus design through to all best faces of the white side veneer sheets, one piece at a time. Double check that you have chosen the correct faces. Now set one of the sheets down on the cutting mat and use the scalpel to remove the first design window. It's best to start with the main central shape (FIG. 10-5, top).

When you have carefully removed the first window, slide a sheet of the harewood under the hole, arrange it for best grain effect, and use the scalpel point to

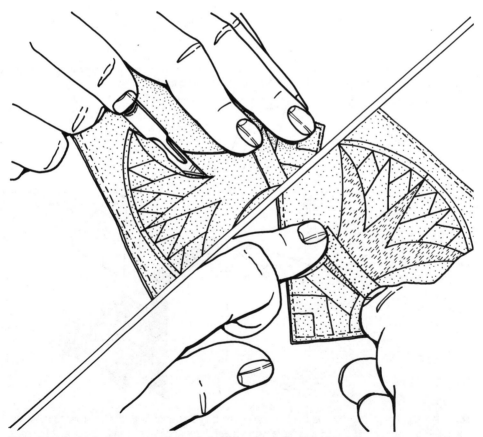

**10-5** Use the scalpel to cut out the central window (top). Position the choice veneer cutout in the window and tape it in place (bottom).

mark through the hole profile. Once the shape is clearly established, remove the veneer to the cutting mat and carefully cut and trim it to shape. Fit the cutout in the window and hold it in place with masking tape (FIG. 10-5, bottom).

Continue working from detail to detail and from sheet to sheet, until all four motifs are complete. This done, carefully remove the tape buildup and replace it with well placed strips of tape on the best face. Think this out carefully when you come to reversing the motifs.

Using the gluefilm and hot iron technique, fit and cut the motif sheets to the four faces of the two angle blocks. With only the bottom and back faces of the pine now left unveneered, fit the three blocks together. Mark in the position of the screws, then pad and protect the veneer faces. Drill pilot holes and countersinks. Smear white PVA glue on all mating surfaces, and fit-and-fix with brass screws (FIG. 10-6). Each bookend needs six screws in all—two from the back through into the motif block, two from the back through into base block, and two up through the base and into the motif block.

Drive the screw heads just below the surface of the wood. Make sure the structure is square and secure and fill the countersink holes with filler. Next, cover the base and the back with black veneer.

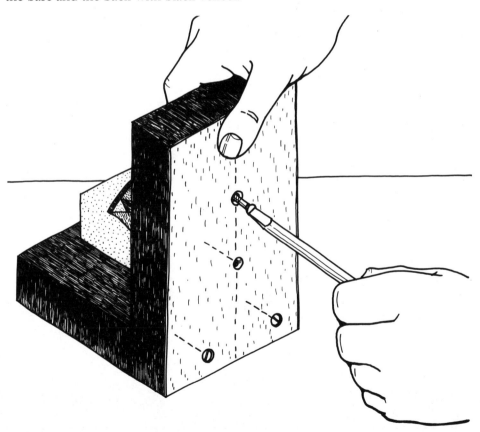

**10-6**  Smear glue on all mating faces and fit and fix the parts with countersunk brass screws.

Finally, when all faces have been veneered, remove all traces of masking tape, rub all faces and edges down with the graded sandpaper, wipe away the dust and lay on several coats of polyurethane varnish.

## HINTS

By *prepared pine*, we mean wood that has been well seasoned, is free from knots and splits, and has been planed so that all surfaces are true and square.

If you can't obtain prepared wood at 1 inch thick, use $7/8$-inch wood and change the project to fit.

You could use wooden dowels rather than screws.

When you are using the hot iron, be careful that you don't overheat the veneer and cause it to split and shrink.

If, when you are ironing on the veneers, the corners start to lift, use a pad of felt to ease the hot veneers over and around the edges.

If you have any doubts about trimming back the various edges, place a straightedge flat against the work before you trim back. Then use a block and garnet paper to rub down the final slight overlap.

# Making a jigsawn inlaid houseboard

Traditional inlay is beautiful! The wood is slowly and carefully trenched and low-ered, the lowered areas are painstakingly filled in with mosaics of exotic wood, and then the whole surface is slowly smoothed off, rubbed down, burnished, and polished.

Not so with this project. Jigsawn inlay is, as they say, a completely different ballgame. The design is drawn out, the wood is cut and fretted with an electric scroll or jigsaw, the cutouts are reversed and glued, and then the work is rubbed down and polished. OK, so jigsawn inlay is limited, but it compensates by being swift and easy.

If you are looking to make a double-sided houseboard (a signboard that can be seen from both sides), and if you are one of those woodworkers who like to go at it fast and furious and have the workpiece all wrapped up and finished by the time the sun goes down, I've got a feeling that this is the project for you. Then again, if you make a really early start and miss out on a few coffee breaks, there's a chance you could have this project three-parts finished before noon.

## CONSIDERING THE PROJECT

Have a look at the project picture and the working drawing (FIGS. 11-1 and 11-2). Note how, at a scale of two grid squares to 1 inch, the board measures 12 × 18 inches.

It is vital with jigsawn inlay that the total design—or at least features within the design—be symmetrical. As you can see, our design is symmetrical—all the cutouts can be turned and reversed to make a counterchange.

However, let's say that you like the idea of the project, but want to go with an asymmetrical design, maybe a tree to the left and a crescent moon to the right. It's easy enough, as long as you make sure that both the tree and the moon are in themselves symmetrical. If the tree and the moon are capable of being turned on their own axis, then no problem—the design will work out. Of course, the draw-ing and cutting needs to be accurate.

Notice in the project picture and working drawing the light-dark counter-change is achieved by cutting out areas and turning them to reveal their other face. Note also how chosen cutouts are not only flipped over, but also shifted so that they occupy the identical mirror-image position on the other side of the verti-

**11-1** Project picture. Note the necessity for a completely symmetrical design.

**11-2**  Working drawing. The scale is two grid squares to 1 inch.

cal axis. For example, if you were cutting a symmetrical face, the eyes would be cut out, flipped over, and then swapped around.

It's actually much easier than it reads. If you do have any problems, take a sheet of paper (black on one side and white on the other), and play around a bit with a pencil and scissors.

## TOOLS AND MATERIALS

In addition to the items listed on p. xi, you need:
- A sheet of 1/2-inch thick, best quality, exterior-grade multicore plywood at 12 × 18 inches.
- Two sheets of straight-grained veneer at 12 × 18 inches in two contrasting colors like mahogany and sycamore.
- Two sheets of gluefilm at 12 × 18 inches.
- A sheet of carbon paper at 12 × 18 inches.
- A sheet of tracing paper.
- The use of an electric flat iron.
- The use of an electric fret/scroll saw; we use a Hegner.
- A pack of fine piercing blades.
- A hand drill with a needle bit.
- A small quantity of exterior-grade filler.
- A tin of clear polyurethane boat varnish.
- A small brush.
- A quantity of white *waterproof* PVA glue.

## THE PROJECT

Take the prepared sheet of 1/2-inch-thick ply board and make sure it is 12 inches wide and 18 inches long. Set a sheet of gluefilm paper-side-up on one side of the plywood, and smooth it over with the electric iron set on medium.

When the film has cooled, peel away the backing paper and position one or other of the two sheets of veneer using tape to hold the veneer at the edges (FIG. 11-3). Protect the veneer with the gluefilm backing paper and work the hot iron back and forth over the surface until the glue has melted. Start at center and work out towards the edges, making sure the work is free from blisters and air pockets. Then remove the paper. Once you have covered one side of the plywood, repeat the procedure and use the other sheet of veneer to cover the other side.

With both sides of the ply now covered with contrasting veneers, take the tracing paper and trace off the lines of the design. Set the board light-side-up on the workbench and sandwich the carbon paper between the tracing paper and the board. Fix it with tape and use a pencil, compass, and ruler to press transfer the lines of the design through to the workpiece (FIG. 11-4).

When all the lines have been very carefully transferred and you have double-checked that the design is symmetrical, bore a pilot hole through the board with the hand drill and small bit. Note the position of the hole on the working drawing (FIG. 11-2).

Set the scroll saw blade through the plywood, correct the blade tension, and

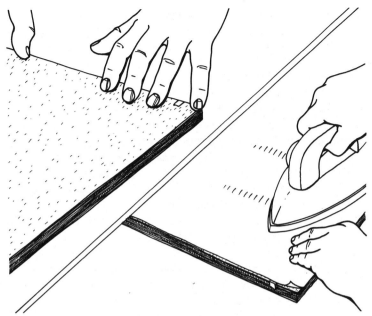

**11-3** When the gluefilm has cooled, peel away the backing paper, position the veneer, and tape it in place (top). Cover the veneer with the backing paper, and work the hot iron from center to side and back and forth (bottom).

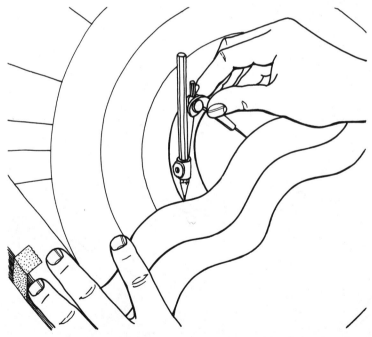

**11-4** Use a pencil, ruler, and compass to press transfer the lines of the design through to the workpiece.

then very carefully cut and fret out all parts that make up the design. Note that, in this instance, we have chosen to saw out the entire center of the board, rather than to cut out individual windows.

When you are sawing out the pieces, make sure that the blade is well tensioned and runs through the wood at right angles to the working face. Of course, you must also stay with the drawn lines (FIG. 11-5).

Having fretted out all the elements of the design, set the frame light-side-up, and carefully replace the cutouts, reversing and counterchanging as you go. Starting at the bottom with the large, wavy-top feature being dark-side-up, continue building light-dark-light-dark, until the design is complete.

When all the pieces have been fitted and counterchanged, cover all the joints on one side with masking tape (FIG. 11-6, top). Smooth the tape into the joints and flip the work over so that it is tape-side-down.

Make sure all the parts are well placed and the gaps look even and equal. Then pipe the PVA glue into the open joints. Wait for the glue to harden, and then top the joints up with glue.

When the glue is dry, clean off any excess, turn the work over, remove all the sticky tape and top up any joints that appear gappy. Do this on both sides. In addition, smear a little filler into all joints on both sides (FIG. 11-6, bottom).

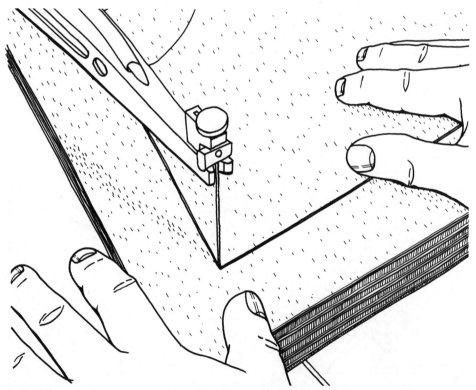

**11-5** Thread the blade through the pilot/starter hole, adjust the tension, and then cut out the main frame.

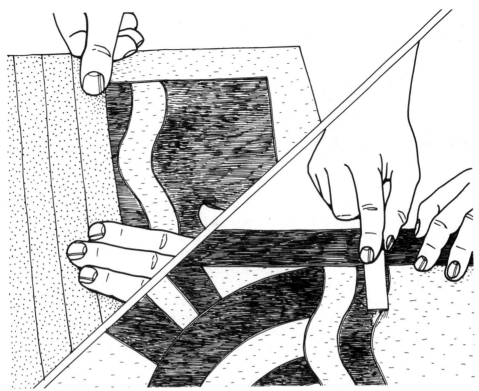

**11-6** Cover one side of the assembly with tape (top). When the piped glue is dry, remove the tape and smear a small amount of filler into the joints (bottom).

Finally, rub all faces and edges down to a good smooth finish, wipe away the dust and debris, and lay on at least two coats of boat varnish.

## HINTS

When you are designing, it is most important that you check and double-check that the whole design and/or features are symmetrical so the design will work. You can check symmetry by reversing the tracing paper and placing it on the transferred lines. All these lines should check out.

When sawing out the design, you can choose to only cut out windows. It is more difficult to cut this way but it is stronger when it has been assembled.

When you are cutting out the design, make sure that the line of cut stays on the drawn line. If you mess up and waver off the line, the pieces might be difficult to fit.

There are any number of exterior grade glues that you might use. You could try one of the gap-filling types. Ask a supplier.

This project is best displayed and hung by being mounted in a metal frame. The large area at the bottom of the design allows for numbers and/or a house name.

# 12
# Decorating picture frame molding

In the context of this book, a *scratch-stock*, sometimes called an *inlay scratch-stock* or a *purfling scratch-stock*, is a wonderfully simple woodworking tool used to cut banding inlay grooves. An electric router or a disc saw might be faster, but just think of the mess and the noise. A scratch-stock, on the other hand, is silent. It is designed to accommodate an infinite number of blade sections and so work a great variety of groove widths and depths. Best of all, a scratch-stock can be made at home or shop bought for a handful of loose change.

The scratch-stock consists of an L-shaped hardwood stock, made up either from two wood thicknesses or from a single piece of wood that has been partially split with a saw kerf. Between the wood thicknesses or in the slot is a small, tooth-like blade. In use, the right-angled wooden stock is butted hard up against the side of the wood to be worked, and then dragged back and forth with a steady scraping action. As the grooves get deeper, so the toothed blade is set lower and lower until the required depth is reached. In the context of an inlay banding, the banding is simply glued and pressed into the trench or groove, and then rubbed down.

If you like decorative picture moldings with inlay bandings, or perhaps wish to decorate the edges of a piece of furniture with inlaid bandings, then this is the project for you.

## CONSIDERING THE PROJECT

Have a good look at the project picture and the working drawings (FIGS. 12-1 and 12-2) and see how the project relates to decorating a shop-bought molding with inlay banding. This project describes: how to use the scratch-stock, how to set the bandings into the grooves, how to finish the surface, and how to use the decorative molding in a mitered-frame context.

Of course, this is not to say that you can't change the project. If you like the idea of inlay bandings, but want to use them to decorate the edge of a table, or a boxlid, for example, simply modify the working details accordingly.

Finally, if you want to try making your own scratch-stock—no problem. A small piece of hardwood, a handful of brass screws, a piece of old hacksaw blade shaped up on a grinding stone, and ten minutes spent rubbing down—what could be easier?

**12-1** Project picture. Molding with decorative inlay banding can be used to frame a mirror or a picture.

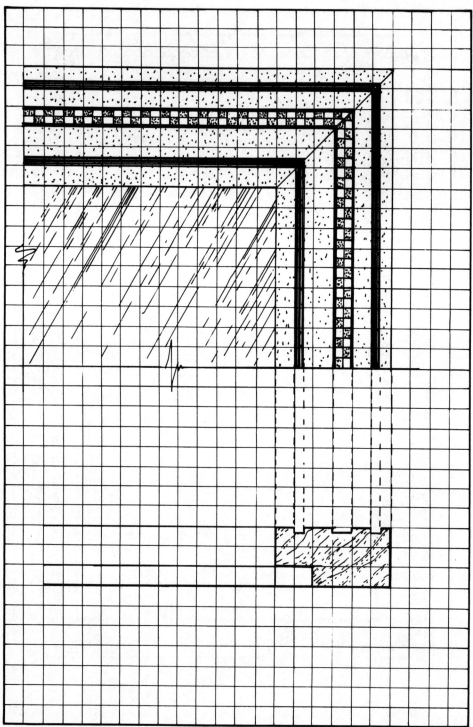

**12-2** Working drawing. The scale is four grid squares to 1 inch.

## TOOLS AND MATERIALS

In addition to the items listed on p. xi, you need:

- A flat-faced, right-angled picture molding/section with a mirror/canvas rebate; go for a smooth-grained easy-to-work wood like lime or box.
- A scratch-stock with blade widths to match the width of your chosen inlay bandings.
- One or more lengths of inlay banding/stringings.
- The use of a workbench.
- A couple of G-clamps.
- A miter block with a 45° setting.
- A small tenon/gents straight saw.
- A lightweight hammer and a handful of small brass pins/nails.
- A set of picture frame clamps.

## THE PROJECT

When you have chosen your molding and bandings, secure one of the lengths of molding to the workbench so that the best face is up and the outside edge/face is

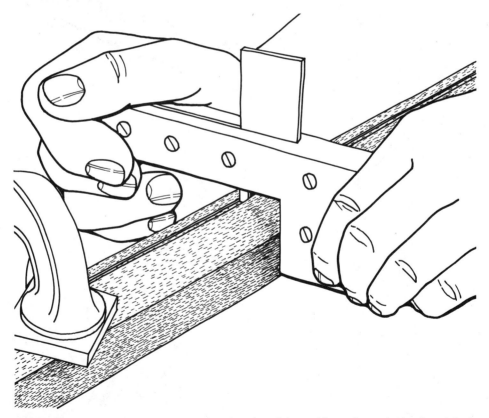

**12-3** Hold the scratch-stock hard up against the edge of the molding to be worked and run it back and forth.

projecting over the edge of the work surface. Have another look at our working drawing (FIG. 12-2), and note how far in from the side edge you want your chosen banding to be. Then set the blade of your scratch-stock accordingly.

Butt the scratch-stock notch block (the inside 90° angle), up against the side of the molding. Be careful to hold the scratch-stock hard up against the wood to be worked and run it repeatedly back and forth with an even, controlled motion (FIG. 12-3).

Because most veneer bandings are usually only about $1/16$ inch thick you need to stop when the groove is just under $1/16$ inch deep. Space and cut grooves to suit your design by moving the toothed blade(s).

When you consider the groove's deep enough, have a trial dry put-together. Ideally, the banding needs to stand slight proud of the ground wood and be a tight push-fit in the groove.

Run the PVA adhesive in the groove, push the banding in place (FIG. 12-4, top), and secure it with masking tape across the center. If the banding is too tight, ease it into place by rubbing it with the face of a clean hammer. Repeat this procedure

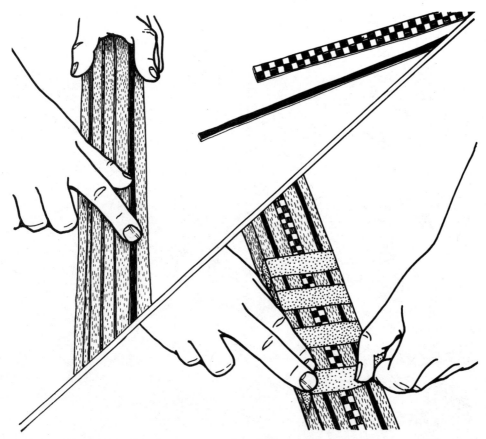

**12-4** Push the banding into the groove so it stands slightly proud of the surface of the molding (top). Secure the strips of banding with tape over and around the molding (bottom).

with all grooves and strips of banding, then secure with more masking tape (FIG. 12-4, bottom). When the glue is dry, remove the tape and rub the inlay bandings down with the sanding block until they are flush with the surface of the molding.

Measure the item that you want to frame and mark the lengths of molding to fit. Allow for miter wastage and remember that frame size relates to the rebate; the picture/mirror needs to be an easy, loose fit within the rebate.

One piece at a time, set the molding in the miter block/box and check that the pencil mark is well aligned with the cutting slot. Allow for the thickness of the saw blade, and make sure that the miter angle is running in the right direction. Then cut the angle (FIG. 12-5). Repeat this procedure with the eight 45° angles that make up the four mitered corners.

Glue the mating faces and, when the glue is tacky, carefully clamp the faces. Drill a pilot hole and hammer in a small strengthening pin. Do this with all four corners (FIG. 12-6, top).

When you have glued and pinned all four corners, put the frame in the clamp and tighten up the twist-cord stick (FIG. 12-6, bottom).

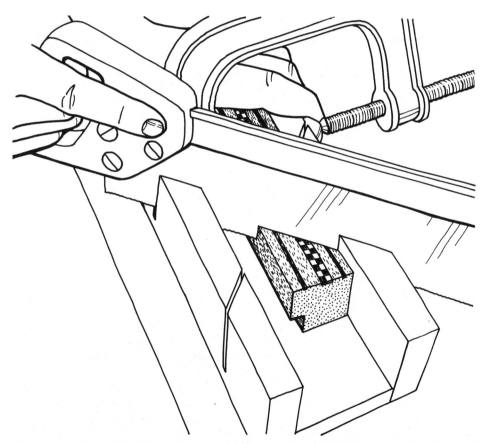

**12-5** Secure the molding with the clamp, locate the saw in the miter block guide, and cut the wood with a careful, even stroke.

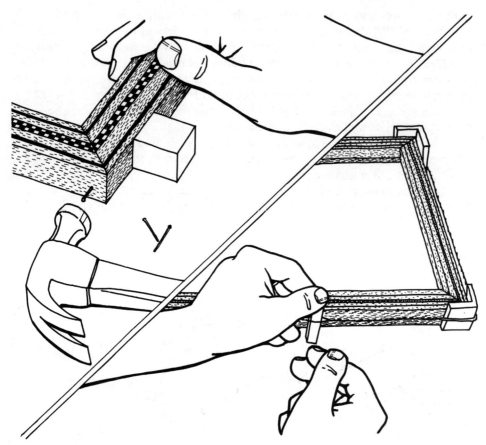

**12-6** Drill a pilot hole and secure with pins (top). Tighten the clamp by twisting the cord stick, making sure that the corners are square (bottom).

Finally, when the glue is dry, remove the frame from the clamps, give the joints a slight rubbing down to remove any traces of glue or rough edges, and lay on a couple of coats of polyurethane varnish.

## HINTS

It is most important that the scratch-stock be butted hard up against the wood being worked. When you are using the scratch-stock, start off by holding at a slight dragging angle. As the work progresses; however, make sure the blade is at right angles to the surface being worked.

Although a scratch-stock will cut right through to the end of a length of molding, it's advisable to work a molding that is slightly longer than needed.

Although a scratch-stock will cut both hard and soft woods, it's best to avoid knotty, sappy, or resinous woods.

Avoid using moldings that have been surfaced with a thin skim of plaster or paint—these will chip.

# Decorating a fire screen with flower picture marquetry

I think it's fair to say that with the craft of marquetry there are almost as many methods and techniques as there are marquetarians. Of course, from book to book and from expert to expert, opinions differ: *"you must never," "you should always," "never," "always," "avoid," "must,"*—the pity is, marquetry often comes across as being a craft governed by many unbending rules.

Generally speaking, our feeling is that there are always at least two ways of skinning a cat. That said, if you are a beginner, it's probably best to try the method as advised first, and then change it to suit your own needs later.

So it is, that although in most instances you should fix the windows with temporary tabs of tape on the best face of the design, in the context of this project, the tape is best placed on the back of the picture. Of course, just prior to gluing, you run strips of tape across the face of the picture and then remove the tape buildup.

Although this particular way of working is contrary to advice given in other projects, the reasoning is simple enough. If, with a marquetry design of this size, you put the temporary tabs of tape on the front of the picture—bear in mind that there are a hundred or so windows—the buildup would be so huge it would hinder progress.

Confused? Best have a go and see how it pans out.

## CONSIDERING THE PROJECT

Have a good look at the project picture and the working drawings (FIGS. 13-1 and 13-2) and see how, at a scale of three grid squares to 2 inches, the screen stands about 24 inches high and 16 inches wide. Note how the background waster is divided to give a horizon line.

One of the best things about working a project of this character is that you can, to a certain degree, use up those hundreds of odds and ends of veneer that you have left over from other projects. Of course, in this project, the cutouts are many, small, and often quite difficult to work. Because the project is quite large, you need to cover the back of the board in a compensating veneer to hold the board flat and stable.

**13-1** Project picture. This traditional design is inspired by a Swedish painted wall motif.

**13-2** Working drawing. The scale is about three grid squares to 2 inches. Note how the waster is divided to give a horizon line.

Finally, this project only describes how to work the marquetry—the idea being that once the marquetry design is finished, you can take the project to completion by making the fire screen, framing the workpiece, and adding simple bracket feet.

## TOOLS AND MATERIALS

In addition to the items listed on p. xi, you need:
- A sheet of good quality 1/2-inch-thick multicore plywood at 16 × 24 inches.
- A sheet of compensating veneer at 18 × 26 inches: go for an easy-to-work wood like sapele.
- A sheet of waster veneer at 18 × 20 inches for the upper half of the design, with the grain running up and down; go for a light-colored veneer like sycamore.
- A sheet of waster veneer at 18 × 8 inches for the lower part of the design with the grain running across the width of the picture; go for a darker veneer like tulipwood.
- A sheet of medium-light-colored veneer for the main vase shape; go for highly figured and fancy veneer like lacewood.
- A good selection of various size off-cuts for the vase, flowers, and foliage. Include green and gray harewoods, dyed black sycamore, pink/red steamed beech, pepper red padouk, sapele, rosewood, purpleheart, sycamore.
- A large sheet each of tracing and workout paper to fit the project.
- A pair of large clamping boards to fit the project.
- Six clamping battens.
- Six G-clamps/cramps.
- A tin of polyurethane varnish.
- A brush.

## THE PROJECT

First take the two main sheets of waster veneer, the sycamore and the tulipwood, square them up and use the knife and the safety ruler to cut through both sheets, making sure the mating edges are straight and flush. (FIG. 13-3, top). Butt-joint the two veneers and fit-and-fix them together with a single strip of masking tape. Don't forget to have the tape on the back or glue-side of the work.

Trace off the lines of the design, using masking tape to hinge the tracing to the top edge of the veneer waster. You will use this tracing constantly during the making stages, so make sure that it is square, centered, and well aligned (FIG. 13-3, bottom).

Pencil-press transfer the traced lines through to the veneer using a soft 2B pencil for the tracing and a hard 3H for the transferring. Start with one of the larger areas—for example, the main body of the vase. Support the workpiece on the cutting mat and use the knife to cut out the first window. Aim for a clean, crisp, well-defined edge. At this stage don't try to work in and around the various

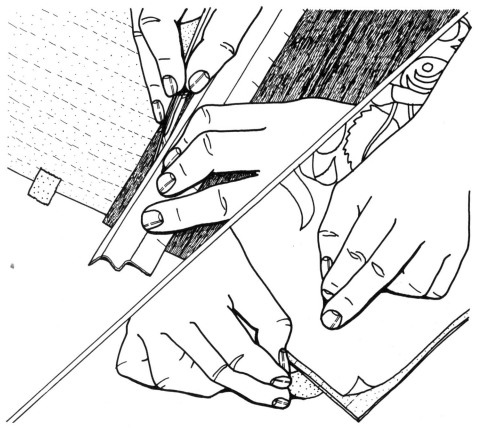

**13-3** Use a knife and safety ruler to cut through both sheets of veneer to give perfectly mating edges (top). Make sure the tracing is square and centered before hinging it to the top edge of the veneer (bottom).

fronds of grass that lap over the vase; just concentrate on the profile, cutting through and across leaves and fronds (FIG. 13-4, top).

Slide the choice sheet of lacewood under the hole, position it for best grain effect, and hold it in place with temporary tabs of masking tape. Use the point of the scalpel around the inside of the window and transfer the shape through to the lacewood (FIG. 13-4, bottom). Hold the knife at 90° and hard up against the side edges of the hole, moving the tape when necessary.

Remove the lacewood to the cutting mat and carefully cut the part-vase shape to a good fit. Continue to hold the knife so that the cut is at 90° to the surface.

Drop the cutout in the window and fit-and-fix it at the back of the work with masking tape. Cut, fit, and fix all the parts of the vase shape. Again, don't worry about the foliage that hangs down over the vase. Rather, have the various horizontal bands running through the full width of the vase by alternating bands of lacewood with a slightly lighter contrasting wood.

When you have completed the vase, retrace the vase profile and the various overhanging fronds and leaves. Cut and fit the leaves that overlap the edge.

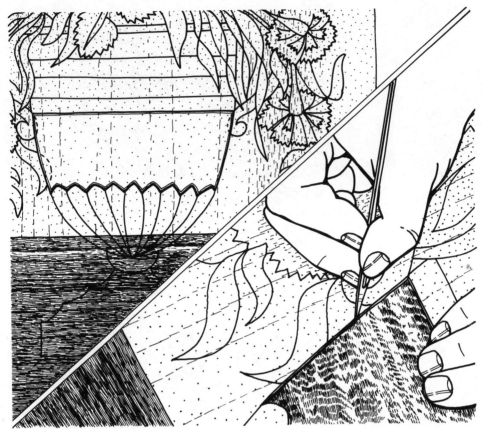

**13-4** When you cut out the first window on the main body of the vase, ignore any overlapping leaves or fronds (top). Transfer the vase shape through to the lacewood by running the point of the scalpel around the inside edge of the window (bottom).

As a general rule, cut out the largest shapes first. For example, you might cut out the whole rose area, replace it with a choice veneer, and then re-establish the lines of the small areas and details.

Continue cutting the windows, selecting choice veneers, cutting pieces to fit, holding the cutouts in place with tape, and so on. Work back and forth across the workpiece until the design is complete.

When you consider your design to be well fitted and fixed, run strips of tape over the whole front of the work and spend time pressing the tape down to hold all the parts in place.

Flip the work over and carefully peel off all the many tabs of tape. To make sure you don't tear any of the delicate veneers, hold the veneer steady with the fingers of one hand while you ease the tape away with the other (FIG. 13-5, top). Flip the work over so that it is tape-side-down, and fill all the open joints with a mixture of fine sanding dust and white PVA adhesive. Work the mixture well into all the cracks and crannies (FIG. 13-5, bottom).

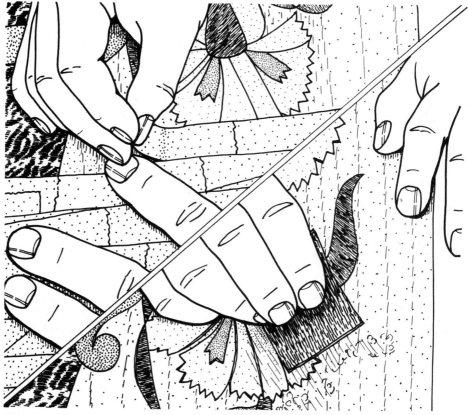

**13-5** Ease the tape away carefully, holding the veneer with the fingers of one hand and pulling the tape away with the other (top). Fill all the open joints with a mixture of fine sanding dust and white PVA adhesive (bottom).

When the filler is dry, rub the surface down with sandpaper to remove all lumps, bumps, and bits. Set the marquetry best-side- or tape-side-down on the work surface and give the plywood board a generous coating of white PVA adhesive. Wait for the glue to become tacky, and then flip the board over and set it down fair and square on the marquetry assembly.

When the marquetry is aligned so that the design is square and centered, and there is an even overlap of waste, slide the workpiece in the clamp and tighten up. Clamp in this order: battens, board, newspaper, plastic sheet, workpiece, plastic sheets, newspaper, board, and battens.

When the glue is dry, take the workpiece out of the clamps, and carefully ease away the strips of masking tape. Trim off the waste veneer overhang, and rub the cut edges down with sandpaper. Repeat the procedure to cover the other side of the board with the compensating sapele veneer.

Rub the face of the work down with the block and graded sandpaper, using first the coarse, then the medium, fine, and super-fine (FIG. 13-6). Clear away all

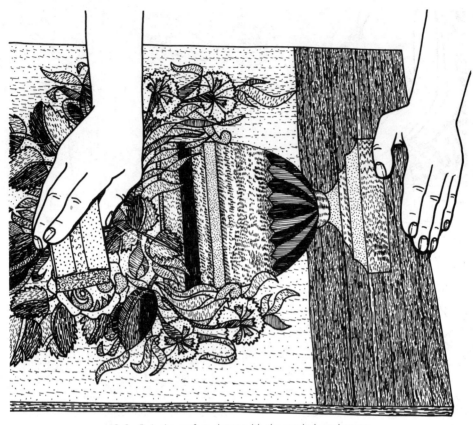

**13-6** Rub the surface down with the graded sandpapers.

the dust and debris, wipe the work down with a turps-dampened cloth, and cover with at least two coats of polyurethane varnish.

Finally, frame the design, set it on a pair of bracket feet of your own making, and the fire screen is finished.

## HINTS

You could use iron-on thermoplastic gluefilm rather than PVA adhesive. If you do, you won't need the clamps and boards, but you will have to work with care so as not to scorch or shrink the cutouts.

If you decide to use a thicker board—for example, 3/4-inch-thick rather than 1/2-inch—you can do without the compensating backing veneer.

If your design is absolutely perfect, why not frame it like a picture and place it with pride over the mantle?

You could perhaps modify the design and use this project in a door-panel context.

# Making a dowel-plugged chopping board

The practice of inlaying or setting small pieces of wood, ivory, shell, stone, and precious metal into a base piece of wood is so old that we really can't put a date on its beginnings. We do know that in ancient Egypt and Greece, all manner of wonderfully exciting inlay designs were created. The Greeks made beautiful coffins inset with precious decorative woods, while the Egyptians favored the making of small caskets and special items of furniture decorated with inlaid ebony, ivory, and semiprecious stones. Even in many so-called, primitive societies, craftsmen still make carved wooden objects, bowls, weapons and the like that are chip-carved and inset with white mastic and mother-of-pearl.

All that apart, when we now think of inlay (sometimes called *intarsia*), we usually have in mind a technique that involves the base wood being variously cut away, lowered or trenched to a depth of between 1/4 and 1/2 inch, the depressions being topped up with more exotic woods, and the surface being leveled and finished.

Dowel-plug inlay, a modern power-tool offshoot of traditional inlay, is special in that it is easy, direct and, most importantly, swift. Holes are first drilled into the base wood, plugs of contrasting wood are cut, glued and hammered into the holes, and finally the surface is cut down and finished.

If you are looking for a swift answer to inlay—one that can be achieved with the minimum of time, effort, and expense—perhaps this is the project for you.

## CONSIDERING THE DESIGN

Have a look at the project drawing and the working drawing (FIGS. 14-1 and 14-2) and see how, at a grid scale of four squares to 1 inch, the finished chopping board measures 6 × 9 inches, and the dowel-plugs are variously 1/4 inch and 1/2 inch in diameter. See how the design relates to a compass-drawn hex-circle. First, a large circle is set out with the compass, the circumference of the circle is stepped off with radius arcs, and straight lines are drawn from the six radius arcs through to the center of the circle. Note how the small twelve-dowel pattern repeats—one 1/2-inch dowel and eleven 1/4-inch dowels—set out using the hex grid as a guide.

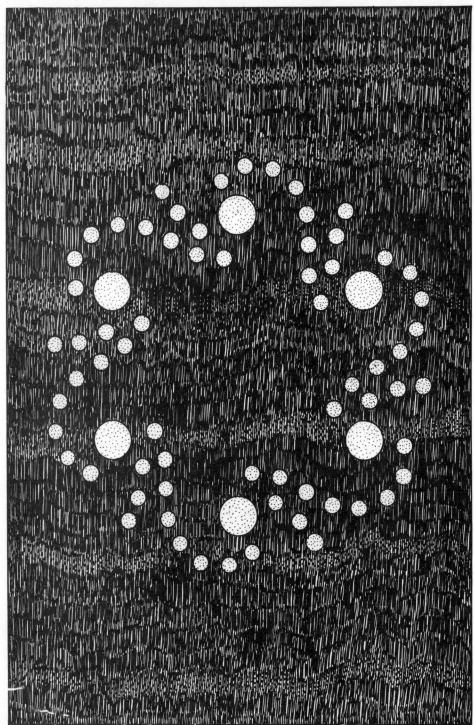

**14-1**  Project picture. Note the two dowel sizes of this dowel-plugged inlay board.

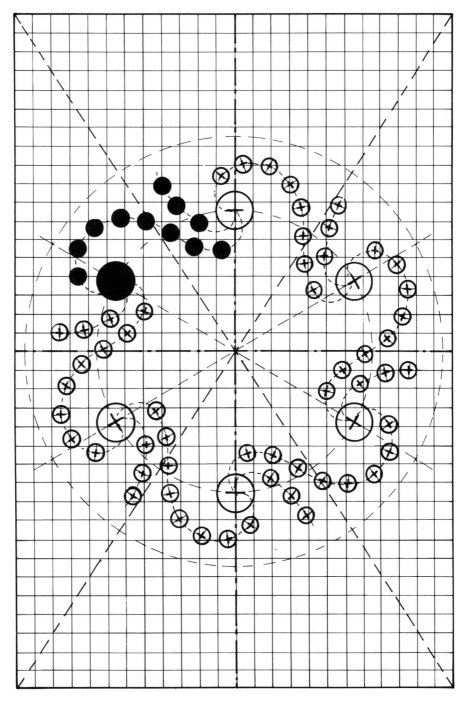

**14-2** Working drawing. The scale is four grid squares to 1 inch. Note the two dowel sizes, $^1/_4$ inch and $^1/_2$ inch.

See how the plugs go right through the wood to give a design on both sides of the slab.

Of course, if you like the technique but want to try something more ambitious, there are any number of exciting options. You could go for a design with a great many more plugs, or maybe a design with many different size dowels. Perhaps you could even have a complex design that uses minute soft brass wire for plugs. You could set the wire plugs in an exotic ebony base and make small items of jewelry. If you do change the design, bear in mind that you need a plug cutter for each drill size, or at least a good selection of ready-made plugs. Consider all the options, and then modify and adjust the project and the design accordingly. Finally, note how the project uses a ready-made $1/4$-inch dowel and a $1/2$-inch plug cutter.

## TOOLS AND MATERIALS

In addition to the items listed on p. xi, you need:
- A slab of 1-inch-thick, dark hardwood at 7 × 10 inches; go for a wood like teak or iroko.
- A slab of $1^{1}/4$-inch-thick, light-colored wood at about 2 × 6 inches for the $1/2$-inch plugs; go for a wood like white maple.
- A couple of lengths of $1/4$-inch-diameter white wood dowel, about 70 inches.
- A sheet each of workout and tracing paper.
- The use of a power drill.
- Two drill bits—one at $1/2$ inch and the other at $1/4$ inch.
- A single $1/2$-inch-diameter plug cutter.
- A hammer.
- A mallet and a square-ended chisel.
- A bottle of vegetable oil
- A piece of fluff-free cotton cloth.

## THE PROJECT

Cut your 1-inch-thick, 7- × 10-inch slab of dark hardwood down to 6 × 9 inches using the square and saw. Aim for a slab that is clean, square-cut, and crisp-edged.

Have a look at the gridded working drawing (FIG. 14-2) and find the center of the slab by drawing crossed diagonals with a ruler and a soft pencil. Set the compass to a radius of $2^{7}/8$ inches, spike the compass on the center point and scribe out a $5^{3}/4$-inch-diameter circle. With the compass still set to the $2^{7}/8$-inch radius, start at 12 o'clock and step off around the circle scribing arcs. Make arc intersections around the clock at 2, 4, 6, 8, 10 and 12 o'clock. Draw radius lines from the center of the circle through each of the six circumference intersections.

Set the compass to a slightly smaller radius of $1^{7}/8$ inches and draw out a $3^{3}/4$-inch-diameter inner circle. Pencil mark the intersections or crossover points of the inner circle and radius lines. Note that they are your main registration points.

Trace off the small twelve-circle pattern—one large circle at $1/2$ inch, and eleven small circles at $1/4$ inch (FIG. 14-3, top).

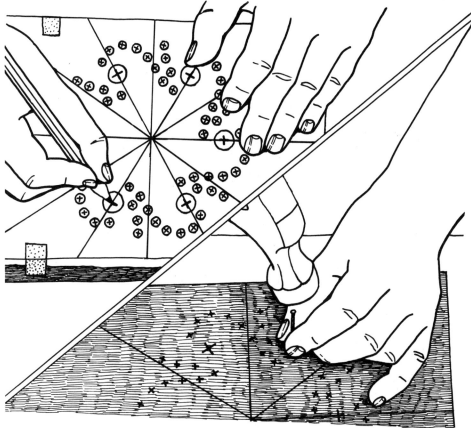

**14-3** Trace off the design, carefully marking in the position of the dowel registration points (top). Use a hammer and a small nail to mark all the plug centers with a small pilot hole (bottom).

With the 6 × 9 inch slab now marked out with the six position-of-large-dowel registration points, take the tracing and align the large ¹/₂-inch plug centers on the registration points and press transfer the circle centers through to the wood.

Continue working around the circle until you have press transferred all the centers of the design. When you are happy with the overall design arrangement, mark all the plug centers with a small pilot hole, using a hammer and a small nail (FIG. 14-3). Then support the board on a waster and clamp it in position on the workbench.

With the electric drill and the two drill bits, bore out all the holes in the design. Aim for clean, crisp-edged holes that run right through the slab at right angles to the working face (FIG. 14-4).

Now, with electric drill and the plug cutter, take the strip of white wood and cut out the ¹/₂-inch-diameter plugs. Cut eight, so you have a couple of spares (FIG. 14-5, top).

Cut the ¹/₄ dowel into 1¹/₄-inch lengths. One at a time, smear glue on the plugs and tap them home. If a plug needs a bit of encouragement, top it with

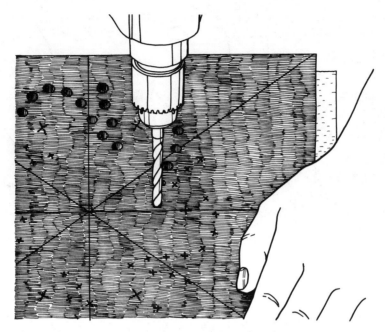

**14-4** Support the workpiece on a slab of waste wood and bore out the dowel holes with a power drill.

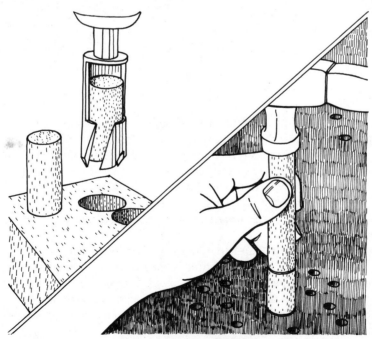

**14-5** Use the plug cutter to cut out the six ¹/₂-inch-diameter plugs (top). Drive the plugs home with a short length of dowel and a hammer (bottom).

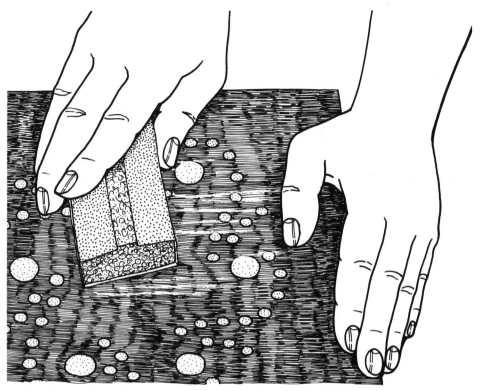

**14-6** Work in the direction of the grain with the graded garnet papers.

another short length of dowel and give it a couple of sharp taps with a hammer. The plugs need to stand out about $1/8$ inch proud on both sides of the slab (FIG. 14-5, bottom).

When the glue is dry, use the chisel and mallet to cut the plugs flush with the surface of the slab.

Finally, use the graded glass/garnet paper to take both sides of the slab to a smooth finish (FIG. 14-6). Round all the edges, rub, and burnish the wood with a drop or two of vegetable oil, and the job is done.

## HINTS

If you decide to modify the design, make sure that the plugs stay about $1/8$ to $1/4$ inch apart.

When you are drilling through the slab, it's important that the drill bit enters and exits at right angles to the working face. If the drill bit is allowed to drift into the wood, the design on the reverse side of the slab will be out of kilter. Holes might even cross and cause plugging problems.

If possible, use a pillar drill or an electric drill held in a stand. Then you will know for sure that the holes are well aligned.

If you decide to use different woods than those named, make sure that they are nontoxic and suitable for a food board.

# 15
# Making a marquetry jigsaw toy

Traditional wooden toys are beautiful—bats, balls, skipping ropes, Noah's Arks, jointed animals, dolls houses, pull-along figures on wheels, and all the rest. But high on our own private list of all-time greats is the plain and simple wooden jigsaw puzzle.

When I was a kid of about 6 years old, I had such a toy. It was made of thick plywood with lots of curvy-edged colored pieces that all fit together to make a collection of farmyard animals. The pieces were color-stained, rather than painted or printed. As I remember, one or two of the pieces were damaged—the pink pig's head had been badly burned, and the cow's back leg was much favored by my baby brother as a chewy-type comfort toy. In all truth, the puzzle was probably nothing more than a disgusting heap of sticky dribble-covered cutouts—but in my eyes, at least, it was a wonderful toy.

## CONSIDERING THE PROJECT

Of all the projects in this book, the rooster, or "cock-a-doodle-doo," jigsaw puzzle is simultaneously the easiest and the most difficult. The puzzle looks to be no more than a dozen or so colored plywood cutouts that link together to make a picture of a chicken—and what could be more straightforward than that! But simply because the profiles are basic and bold, it is all the more important that the cutouts be perfectly sawn and the colored veneers be fitted and finished to a high standard.

Have a good look at the project picture and the working drawing (FIGS. 15-1 and 15-2) and see how, at a grid scale of four squares to 1 inch, the puzzle measures 6 × 9 inches. Note that the puzzle is made up of two layers of ply, with the surround being bonded to the base to make a double thickness recess.

When you have studied the working drawing, take your workout paper and colored pencils to see if you can improve our design. You could make the puzzle much larger, make smaller and more complex pieces, or go for a different image, like a jungle animal. There are any number of exciting possibilities.

## TOOLS AND MATERIALS

In addition to the items listed on p. xi, you need:
- Two pieces of white-faced 1/4-inch-thick multicore plywood at 7 × 10 inches.

**15-1** Project picture. Note the way the various pieces have been worked so that grain and color are used to best effect.

**15-2** Working drawing. The scale is four grid squares to 1 inch. Note the black, X-marked starter hole.

- A pack of mixed-color dyed-wood veneers. There are ten or so pieces in the pack, each measuring about 6 × 4 inches; go for colors like, plum, brown, green, pink, blue, orange, yellow, black, red, and gray.
- A large sheet of veneer at 7 × 10 inches, for the puzzle surround; go for an exciting grainy veneer like birch, ayan, moiree, or sapele.
- A sheet of tracing paper.
- A fretwork saw with a pack of spare blades.
- A set square.
- A hand drill with a fine needle drill bit.
- A sheet of thermoplastic gluefilm at about 24 × 24 inches.
- The use of a hot iron.
- A tin of grain sealer.
- A tin of polyurethane varnish.
- A 1-inch paint brush.

## THE PROJECT

Take the two 7 × 10 inch sheets of ¹/₄-inch plywood and variously saw, cut, and trim, until they are clean-edged, measure 6 × 9 inches, and square and well

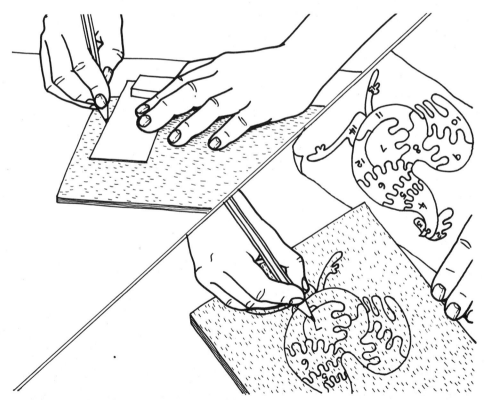

**15-3** Use the pencil, ruler, and set squares to achieve right-angled 6- × 9-inch form (top). Number the various shapes on both the tracing and the wood (bottom).

matched (FIG. 15-3, top). When you have achieved a good crisp master design, take a pencil tracing. With the best of the two boards, carefully pencil-press transfer the traced design through to the working face. Use a pencil to number the various shapes on both the tracing and the wood, on the best face (FIG. 15-3, bottom).

Check that all is correct and drill a small starter hole. Use a Hegner-type scroll saw to fret out the various shapes (FIG. 15-4).

With each of the plywood cutouts carefully numbered on the best face, give them a swift rub-over with the glass paper to remove rough edges. Be careful not to round-over the edges.

Sit down with the colored veneers and the design, and decide how you want the colors to be. Then decide on the direction of the grain. See if you can use the character of the grain to extend the design, maybe to suggest feathers or leg scales. Chalk-number the veneer on its best face.

Cut a piece of veneer to fit each of the cutouts, one piece for each of the plywood cutouts that make up the rooster puzzle, and a large piece for the surround. Pair each piece of colored veneer with a piece of gluefilm. One piece at a time, take a matching threesome of veneer, gluefilm, and plywood cutout.

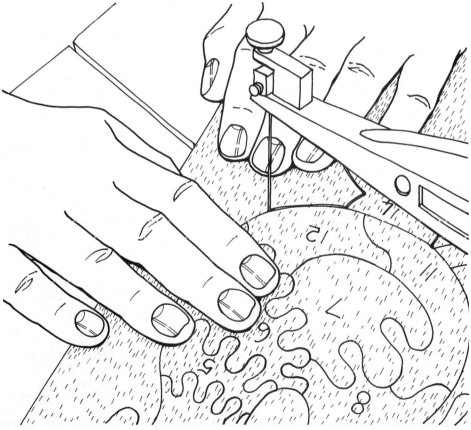

**15-4** Use an electric scroll saw to fret out the shapes, aiming for crisp angles and smooth curves.

Set the veneer best-face-down on the work surface, position the gluefilm paper-side-up on the veneer, and touch it here and there with the iron set on medium, to tack the film in place (FIG. 15-5, top left). When the glue is cool, carefully peel off the backing paper (FIG. 15-5, top right).

Set the plywood cutout best-face-up on the bench, and make sure the grain of the veneer runs in the right direction. Set the veneer glue-side-down on the cutout and cover it with the backing paper to protect it from scorching. Then work slowly over the surface with the hot iron until the gluefilm has melted (FIG. 15-5, bottom). Continue until all the plywood cutouts and the surround have been covered with veneer.

When the glue has cooled, peel off the backing paper and check the work over. Make sure the veneer is well stuck down and free from air pockets.

One piece at a time, set the plywood cutouts veneer-side-down on the cutting board, and use the fine-point scalpel to cut away the waste veneer. Run the blade hard up against the edge of the ply to achieve a clean, crisp, right-angled

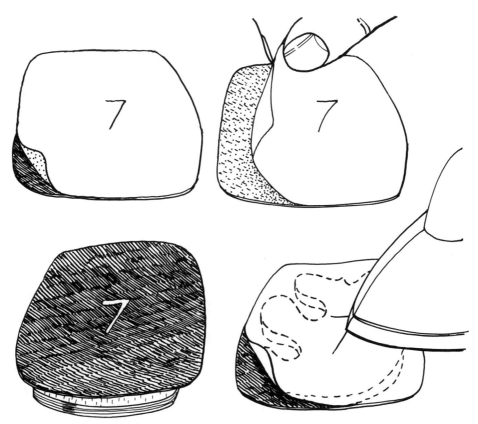

**15-5** Set the veneer best-face-down on the work surface, and position the gluefilm paper-side-up on the veneer, (top left). When the glue is cool, carefully peel away the backing paper (top right). Cover the veneer with the backing paper and work the hot iron back and forth until the glue has melted (bottom).

cut. When all the pieces have been trimmed, lay on a generous coat of grain sealer to protect the color. Wait for the sealer to dry and then rub down *twice*.

Use the fine-grade garnet paper to rub down the veneer face and the ply edges. Slightly round the topmost edges until the whole puzzle is a good, smooth-to-the-touch fit.

Put the puzzle cutouts to one side, and use the PVA glue to fix the surround to the base board (FIG. 15-6). Glue, fit, and apply pressure to the two boards. Make sure that the glue doesn't ooze into the rooster-shaped recess.

When the glue is dry, remove all the bits of glue, put on a last coat of sealer, rub the whole thing down with the graded glass paper and brush away the dust. Finally, take the cutouts, one piece at a time, and lay on at least two coats of varnish. Make sure that you varnish all faces and edges.

## HINTS

One or two of the puzzle pieces are quite small. If you are at all worried about toy-sucking toddlers swallowing the pieces, then consider adjusting the design for larger cutouts. For example, the head, beak, and comb could be all one piece.

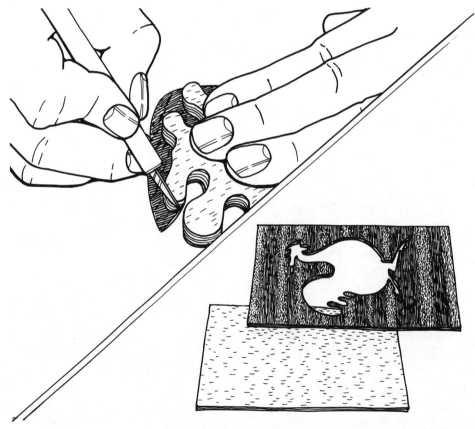

**15-6**  Trim the veneer overlap (top). Glue the cutout surround to the baseboard (bottom).

If you don't much like the idea of trimming the veneer once it has been mounted on the finished cutout, adjust the project to first cut and mount the veneer shapes on the plywood, and then do the sawing.

You could reshape the project to have, for example, lots of smaller farmyard animals all fitting together to make a picture. Each cutout could be a different animal—a pink pig, a brown dog, a white sheep, a yellow duckling, and so on.

# 16

# Decorating a chest in the Nonesuch tradition

**N**onesuch is the name commonly given to a group of sixteenth-century English inlay chests. Nonesuch chests are characterized by having a central palace-like motif surrounded by strips, frames, and borders of geometrical, parquetry-like designs. The palace motif supposedly draws its inspiration from King Henry VIII's fabled pleasure palace of Nonesuch. It's a beautiful thought.

The curious thing is that all these chests—we've seen about five or six—look as if they were mass-produced or made by the same hand. As like as not, they were all made in the same workshop. The border designs are built up from little geometrical repeats—small squares, triangles, diamonds, and bars of wood that look, on close inspection, to be about 1/4-inch thick. It's not really possible to positively identify the wood, but the grain is close and smooth, and the colors range from a pale yellow through to light brown, dark brown, and dyed black.

## CONSIDERING THE PROJECT

Have a good long look at the project picture and the working drawing (FIGS. 16-1 and 16-2). Although the chests are traditionally decorated with inlay, we have modified the techniques and used window marquetry for the palace motif and strip parquetry for the borders. As for wood types, best use easy-to-work, straight-grained veneers like dyed black sycamore, white sycamore, yellow/cream boxwood, and maybe a pink-brown fruitwood like pear.

See how, at a scale of two grid squares to 2 inches, the design relates to an area 12 × 18 inches. Although we see the design as being repeated and set side-by-side to cover a chest top measuring 18 by 24 inches, there's no reason at all why you shouldn't change the scale and the proportions to suit your own needs.

## TOOLS AND MATERIALS

In addition to the items listed on p. xi, you need:
- A surface to cover—a chest lid or a table top.
- A good selection of straight-grained veneers—a piece of sycamore at about 8 × 15 inches for the central motif waster, and two pieces each at 7 × 19

**16-1** Project picture. This project draws its inspiration from a traditional Nonesuch inlay design. Note the characteristic palace details and the strip parquetry borders.

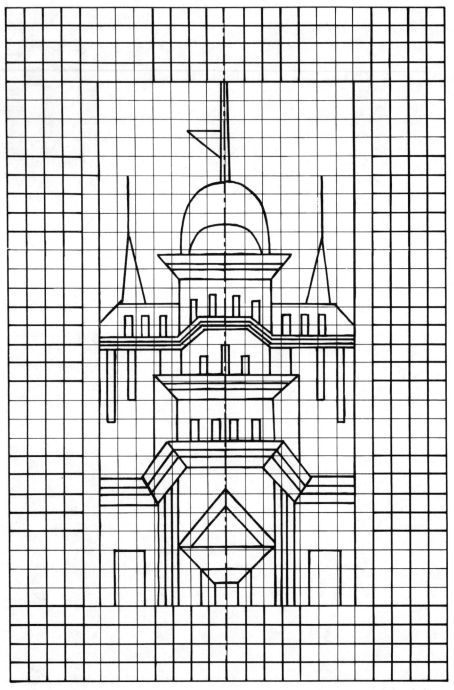

**16-2** Working drawing. The scale is two grid squares to 1 inch. We have repeated the design and have used it on a chest top that measures 18 × 24 inches.

inches of yellow/cream boxwood, brown sapele, and black dyed sycamore.

- A tin of impact adhesive.
- A sheet of tracing paper.
- A sheet of wet-strength tissue paper at about 7 × 14 inches.
- A tube/stick of quick-dry paper-to-paper paste.
- A sheet of strong, smooth brown paper at 13 × 18 inches.
- A small rubber roller.
- A tin of beeswax polish.

## THE PROJECT

Trace off the central motif and carefully press transfer the traced lines through to the sheet of tissue paper. Use the quick-dry paste to fix the tissue to the sheet of waster veneer. Make sure that the tissue is well stuck and smoothed out, and have the grain running from top to bottom of the design. Allow for a generous margin of all-around waste (FIG. 16-3, top).

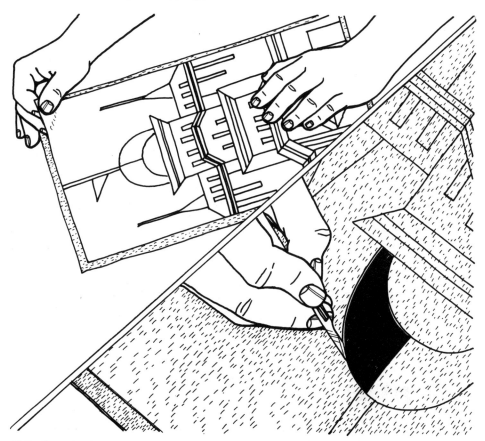

**16-3** Paste the tissue paper design directly to the sheet of veneer (top). Run the scalpel around the inside edge of the window and mark the shape through to the piece of black veneer (bottom).

Bearing in mind that a good part of the waster will be left into position for the sky and bits of the palace, cut away the top central dome with the scalpel, and place a piece of black veneer behind the hole. Hold this in position with two temporary tabs of tape.

Run the point of the scalpel around the inside of the hole and mark the shape through onto the black veneer, using the hole as a template (FIG. 16-3, bottom). With the shape carefully marked through to the black veneer, remove the tabs of tape, cut out the dome shape, making several passes with the knife.

When the shape has been successfully cut out, fit it into the window and hold it in place with a few tabs of masking tape on the face side (FIG. 16-4). NOTE: You can, if you so wish, split the dome shapes and have them made from two mirror-matched veneers.

Continue working back and forth over the design, all the while cutting out windows and filling in with selected veneers. Trim back edges to pattern size and tape on the black strips at either side of the palace. When you have cut and fitted all the windows, remove some of the tape buildup and refix with single strips of tape. Put the finished central motif to one side.

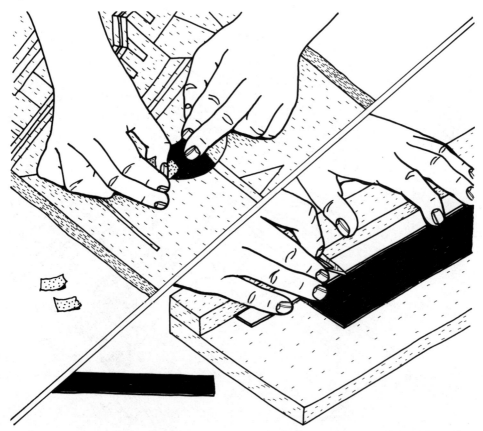

**16-4** Set the cutout in the window and fix it with tape (top). Cut the veneer into 1/2-inch-wide strips; best use a fixed width guide and a cutting board with a backstop (bottom).

Now take a sheet each of dyed black sycamore and boxwood, and use a pencil, safety ruler, and knife to cut the veneer down into $1/2$-inch wide strips. Use a cutting board with a fixed-width guide strip/jig (FIG. 16-4, bottom).

Take two strips each of the black sycamore and the yellow boxwood and set them side-by-side so that the color sequence goes black-yellow-black-yellow. Run strips of masking tape down the joints, and make four such bands.

Measure, mark, and cut off from the end of the 2-inch-wide bands—56 strips at $1/2$ inch wide, and 12 blocks at 2 inches. (FIG. 16-5, top).

Have another look at the working drawing and the project picture, then reverse and turn the strips one to another in order to make the checkered counterchange border design. Cut, trim and fit the border around the central palace motif, and have the whole assembly held with straps and tabs of masking tape on the face side.

With the workpiece now being held together as a single sheet, take the contact adhesive and spread a good, even coat on both the back of the veneer and the suface to be covered. Use a scrap of veneer as a spreader and make sure that you cover all the corners and edges (FIG. 16-5, bottom).

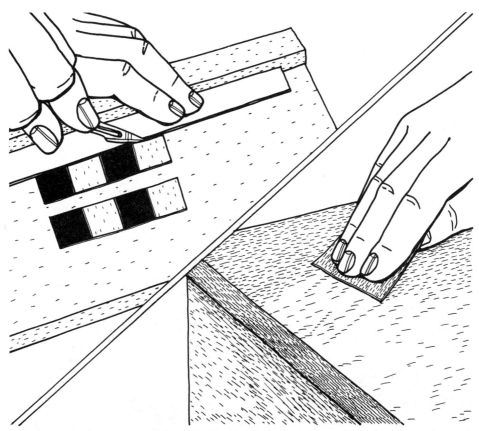

**16-5** Cut the $1/2$-inch strips and the 2-inch-wide blocks ready for assembly (top). Spread a good, even coat of contact adhesive over the surface to be covered (bottom).

When the film of glue is touch-dry, cover the groundwork with the sheet of brown paper and set the veneer glue-side-down and in position on the paper. Being very careful that the glue-covered surfaces don't come into contact before you are ready, make sure that the design is well aligned. Pin the veneer at one end.

At the same time, gradually withdraw the brown paper from between the sheets and run the roller over the veneer (FIG. 16-6). Work the roller from center to sides, all the while making sure that the glue-covered surfaces come together without trapping pockets of air. Remove the masking tape and use a spirit-dampened cloth to wipe away all traces of tape and adhesive residue.

Rub the work down to a good, smooth finish, and clean up all the dust and debris. Trim back all the edge overlaps. Finally, lay on a generous coat of wax polish—work it into all the cracks and crannies—and burnish the wood to a good, hard finish.

## HINTS

When you are choosing veneers, best go for smooth, straight-grained types like boxwood, sycamore, and fruitwoods.

**16-6** Gradually withdraw the slip paper from between the veneer assembly and the chest top. Apply pressure with a roller and work from center to side, being careful that you don't trap air pockets.

When you are cutting the wood into strips, make sure that the knife blade doesn't run into the grain and wander away from the line of cut.

There is no going back once the glue-covered surfaces come into contact, so make sure that the alignment is correct before you pull out the slip paper.

You could give the chest a generous edge strip of mahogany; go for a slightly round-edge section.

If you plan to have this chest in a sticky-finger-licking toddler's room, you should probably go for a varnish finish rather than the wax. Protect the veneers with three or four coats of clear polyurethane varnish.

# 17
# Decorating a surface with inlay tiles

**S**awn plug inlay and strip inlay are both good, sound techniques in their own right. But bring them together and they become a duo-technique that is capable of great and varied expression. Used as a single method of inlay-marquetry decoration, this delightful hybrid is much akin to oyster-shell veneering, plug inlay, Tunbridge work and butcher's block inlay. Just like these four tried-and-trusted traditional techniques, the plug-strip method results in a surface that is made up of end-grain wood. Therefore, when the primary block is drilled, plugged, laminated, and sliced, and the slices are mounted tile-like, the face of each tile shows up as end-grain.

The secret of success with the plug-strip method is in the initial planning and bringing together of the various woods, in the arrangement of the tiles, and in the finishing. Best go for simple, straight-grained contrasting woods and a basic lamination layout. If you want to decorate a broad, flat surface with simple geometrical forms, then this is the project for you.

## CONSIDERING THE PROJECT

Have a look at the project picture and the working drawing (FIGS. 17-1 and 17-2), and see how the initial pre-cut block is made up from a drilled and dowel-plugged square section sheathed with thin contrasting strips. See how all the elements relate to basic, prepared, off-the-shelf sections, with the dowel being 3/8 inches in diameter, the square section measuring 3/4 × 3/4 inches, and the strips measuring 1/8 × 7/8 inches.

Note how the initial pre-cut block measures 1 × 1 inches square. See also how the checker-square placing of the tiles results in a beautifully simple and direct basketweave design. The sum total project is easy enough, even though the block does need to be drilled with great care. The best advice is to only try to drill short lengths at a time—1 1/2 to 2 inches—set the wood in a vice, and use a clamp or jig to make sure that the drill is well centered and square. Spend some time at the pre-drill stage making sure that the drill isn't going to wander off-center. Bear in mind when you are ordering wood that each sawn slice needs to be about 1/8 inch thick, and allow for wastage.

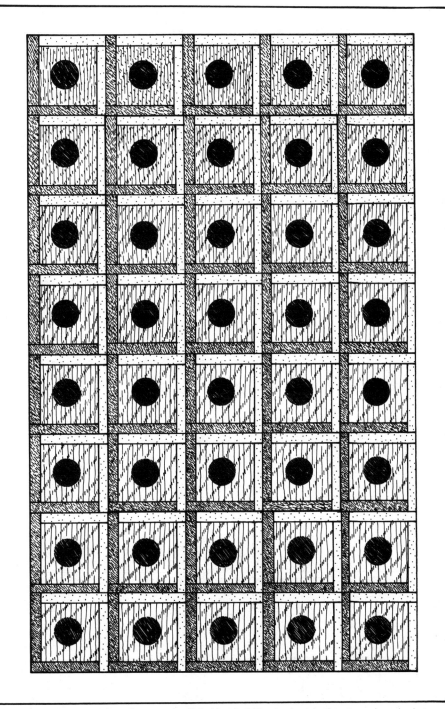

**17-1** Project picture. Note the way the little identical tiles come together to make a basketweave design.

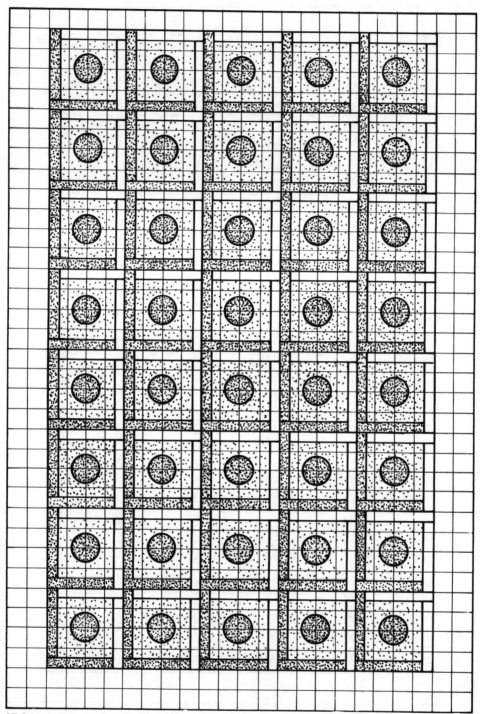

**17-2** Working drawing. The scale is four grid squares to 1 inch. Note how the sheathing needs to be arranged.

## TOOLS AND MATERIALS

In addition to the items listed on p. xi, you need:
- A length of medium-light-colored wood at $3/4 \times 3/4$ inches square for the central core.
- A length of $3/8$-inch-diameter dark wood dowel for the plug.
- Four lengths of $1/8$- $\times$ $7/8$-inch strip; two dark and two light.
- A drill and a $3/8$-inch-diameter bit.
- A bench hook and a small straight saw.
- A hammer.
- The object to decorate—go for a broad, flat surface like a table board or box.
- A pair of clamping boards.
- A quantity of newspaper.
- A couple of sheets of thin plastic.
- Four clamping battens.
- Four G-clamps/G-cramps.
- A metal scraper.
- A tin of beeswax polish.

## THE PROJECT

Have a good look at the working drawing (FIG. 17-2), then check your wood over to make sure it is free from splits, warps, and other flaws. Also make sure all edges, faces and angles are straight and true.

Take the $3/4$- $\times$ $3/4$-inch core piece, mark out one end with crossed diagonals, and fix the center point. Set the wood end-up in a vice, clamp, or jig, and carefully sink a $3/8$-inch-diameter hole. It's very important that the hole runs square and true through the wood (FIG. 17-3, top).

Take the dark-wood, $3/8$-inch-diameter dowel, rub it down slightly, brush it with PVA adhesive and tap it home into the central core hole (FIG. 17-3, bottom).

Having noted the way the four $1/8$-inch-thick strips are arranged, glue all mating surfaces, set the strips in position around the core, wipe away excess glue, and bind the whole arrangement with masking tape (FIG. 17-4, bottom). When the glue is dry, remove the tape and scrape off all runs and dribbles of hard glue. One side at a time, put the piece in a muffled vice and use a block and sandpaper to rub the wood down to a smooth, square-cornered finish.

Set the wood in the bench hook and use the straight saw to cut the wood down into $1/8$-inch slices (FIG. 17-5). You could build a little slice-thickness jig with clamps and scrap wood. Pencil mark the slices on the best face and have a dry-run fitting. Make sure that each tile is identically placed.

When you are happy with the overall arrangement, brush a generous amount of PVA adhesive over the surface to be decorated, and set the tiles into position. Position the work between boards and clamp up in this order: two battens, a board, a layer of newspaper or felt, a sheet of plastic, the workpiece, a sheet of plastic, the newspaper, the board, and the two battens (FIG. 17-6, top).

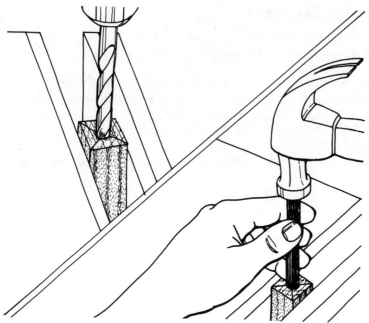

**17-3** Set the wood end-up in the vice and carefully sink a ³/₈-inch-diameter hole (top). Tap the ³/₈-inch-diameter dowel into the central core hole (bottom).

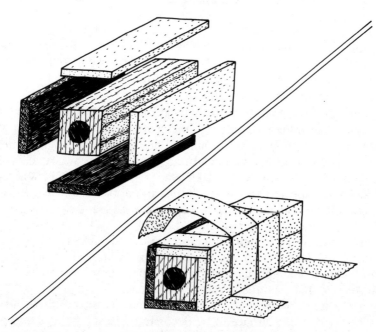

**17-4** Note carefully how the four ⁷/₈- × ¹/₈-inch strips are arranged around the central block (top). Glue all mating surfaces, set the strips into position, and bind the assembly with masking tape (bottom).

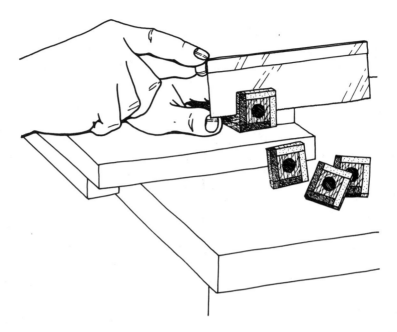

**17-5** Butt the workpiece hard up into the bench hook and use the straight saw to cut the wood down into 1/8-inch-thick slices.

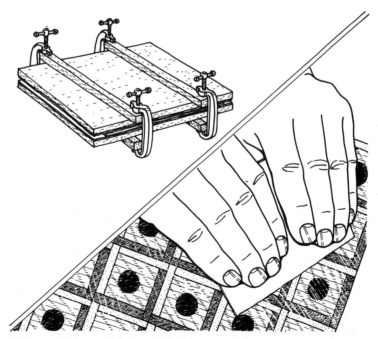

**17-6** Put the work in the clamp until the glue is dry (top). Use a metal scraper to work the surface down to a good smooth finish (bottom).

When the glue is dry, remove the clamps and set about cleaning off all the hard blobs of excess glue. Use the metal scraper to work the surface down to a good finish (FIG. 17-6, bottom).

Having variously worked the scraper with and across the grain, use the graded sandpaper and block to rub the surface down to a good, smooth finish.

Finally, take the beeswax polish and a smooth fluff-free cotton cloth, and burnish the work to a high-sheen finish.

## HINTS

If you can't obtain a prepared dark wood dowel, you could either stain the dowel or change things around a bit to have a light wood dowel and a dark 3/4- × 3/4-inch core.

When you come to gluing up, make sure that all mating surfaces come together for a good fit.

If you cut slices thinner than 1/8 inch, there is a chance the slices will cup and split.

When you are clamping up, make sure that the tiles don't twist out of alignment. It's best to tighten up the clamps, ease off to check the arrangement, and then re-clamp.

# Making and decorating a wall clock

**D**iamond matching selected veneers is an exciting—if slightly finger-twisting—technique. Of course, window marquetry is, as we hope you know by now, wonderfully easy and uncomplicated. Put these two techniques together and serve them up in the form of a wall clock, and you have a project that presents a special challenge. Better still, build into this talent-stretching twosome an intricate motif that draws inspiration from the uniquely beautiful and striking work of the Russian artist Ivan Yakovlecvich Bilibin (1876–1942), and you're well on the way to having a project that is as challenging and as multifaceted as you care to make it.

The clock movement aspect of the project, is no problem. Modern, lightweight, battery-run quartz movements are so efficient, so easy to fit, and so inexpensive, that the clock part can be managed with a minimum of effort and know-how. A single drilled hole, a couple of screws, push-fit the hands, and the clock movement is fitted. What could be easier?

So if you're looking for a challenge and if you like cutting and working small, intricate details, this is the project for you.

## CONSIDERING THE PROJECT

Have a look at the project picture, the working drawings (FIGS. 18-1 and 18-2), and the materials list, to see how this project is—all at the same time—easy, complicated, a challenge, colorful and beautiful. Diamond matching is a great way of joining and presenting veneers, not only because you use quite narrow strips of veneers, but also because the use of the technique results in a strikingly attractive 45° four-square diamond pattern. If you set the clock at the center of the diamond-match pattern, the whole design pulls your eye towards its center.

## TOOLS AND MATERIALS

In addition to the items on p. xi, you need:
- A sheet of 3/8-inch-thick plywood at 6 × 9 inches.
- Four consecutive matching sheets of rosewood at about 5 inches wide and 12 inches long use Indian rosewood.
- A 45° metal set square.
- An assorted pack of small veneer off-cuts for the motif. Include a golden colored African satinwood for the bell shapes and flowers, a delicate pink

**18-1** Project picture. Note how the ground veneer has been diamond-matched and the motif mirror-imaged.

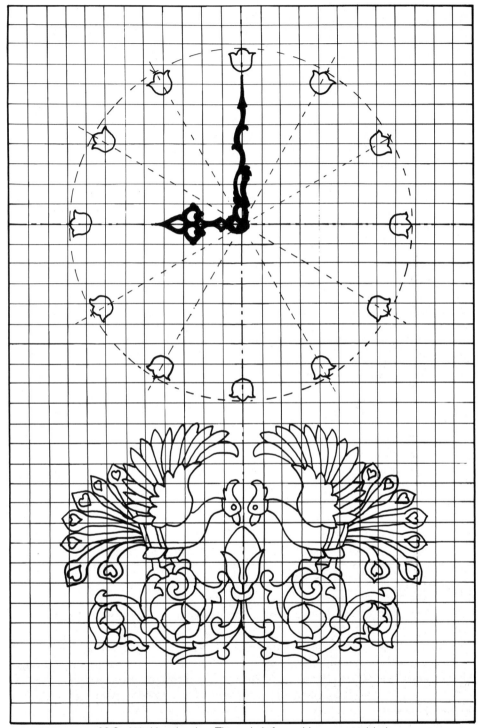

**18-2** Working drawing. The scale is four grid squares to I inch.

pearwood for the twined stems and birds tails, a small piece of rich ginger/ brown padouk for the heart shapes, the head, feet, and other small details, cream boxwood for the wings, eyes, and beak, and a white birch for the bird's body, wing feathers, and leaves.
- A sheet each of tracing and workout paper.
- A small, inexpensive battery-driven quartz clock movement, with fancy hands to fit.
- A hand drill with a drill bit to fit the clock spindle, probably about 1/4 to 1/2 inch. (See the clock's own fitting details.)
- A couple of clamping boards.
- A couple of sheets of plastic film.
- A clamping press weight; we use a plastic bag full of damp sand.
- A tin of furniture polish—best if it's beeswax.

## THE PROJECT

Take the four consecutive 5 × 12 inch sheets of rosewood, make sure that the edges and ends are square, and strap them together with the masking tape. Using the knife at 45° square and the safety ruler, cut through the four-leaf stack to make a 45° rhomboid. Don't try to slash through the veneers at a single stroke. Instead, do it little by little, with many well-placed, small cuts (FIG. 18-3, top).

With the sheets still in consecutive order, pair them up, open them out, butt them edge to edge, and fix them with strips of masking tape. You should now have two arrow shapes with the grain running to the point of the arrow.

Place the arrow shape on the cutting mat and set the safety ruler across the width of the arrow, from shoulder to shoulder. Make sure that the central crossover is at a right angle with the center line, and then cut the arrow shape in half. Do this with both arrows (FIG. 18-3, bottom left).

You should now have four pieces, two triangles and two winged shapes. Rearrange the pieces so that the two triangles touch along the hypotenuse lines (the sides opposite the right angle), and so that the winged shapes enclose what is now a central diamond. If all is well and as described, the 90° corners of the two winged shapes should form the main corners of what is now a long rectangle (FIG. 18-3, bottom right).

Having made sure that all edges are carefully butt-jointed and tacked in place with tape, turn the work over and fit-and-fix with strips of tape. Then remove all the small tabs of tape from the best side.

Use the metal 45° set square, the safety ruler, and the scalpel to cut the assembly down in size so that it measures slightly over 6 × 9 inches, and so that the diamond center/clock center occurs about 3 inches down from the top.

Trace off the bird design, using masking tape to hinge the tracing fair and square within the diamond match assembly. Hinge the tracing along the top edge and pencil-press transfer the lines of the design through to the workpiece (FIG. 18-4). Lift the tracing to check that all the lines have been transferred; keep the tracing hinged for quick reference.

Because rosewood is relatively dark, you should spend time making sure the

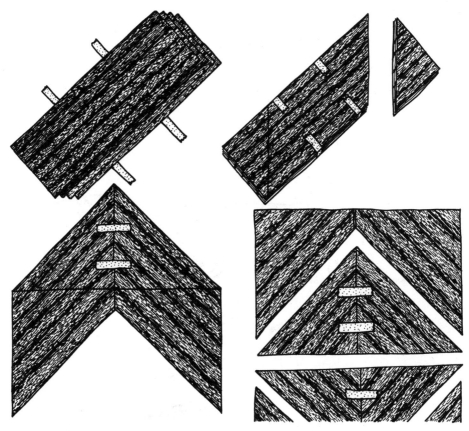

**18-3** Cut through the four-leaf stack so as to make a 45° rhomboid (top). Make sure the central crossover is at 90° to the center axis and cut the arrow shape in half at the shoulder line (bottom left). Rearrange the pieces so that the two triangles touch along the hypotenuse and the winged shapes enclose what is now the central diamond (bottom right).

lines of the design are clear, crisp, and well established. If necessary, go over the transferred lines with a hard pencil.

Starting with one of the large primary forms like one of the birds bodies, cut out the first window. When you have cut and carefully trimmed back the first window to the drawn line, slide your chosen veneer under the hole, arrange it for best grain effect, and fit with temporary tabs of masking tape on the back.

Transfer the window shape through to the veneer by scratching around the sides of the hole with the point of a scalpel. Do this slowly and carefully a couple of times, until the outline is clearly established. Make sure that you hold the knife upright so the blade is at 90° to the face. Then remove the veneer to the cutting mat, and cut out the small shape. Make sure the scalpel blade is super-sharp.

Fit the cutout in the window by gently nudging it in place with the point of the blade, (FIG. 18-5, top) and hold it in place with small tabs of tape. Continue until all the areas of the drawn design have been replaced with choice veneers.

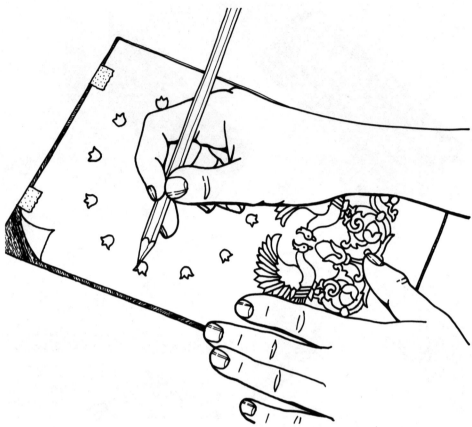

**18-4** Hinge the tracing fair square within the diamond match assembly along the top edge and pencil-press transfer the lines of the design.

Make sure that the twelve little motifs that make up the clock ring are perfectly placed in relationship with the center of the clock and with each other.

When the whole design has been cut and worked to your satisfaction, tape the best face with single, well-placed strips that run the length of the workpiece and remove the tape from the back (FIG. 18-5, bottom).

Set the prepared 6 × 9-inch-plywood board down on the newspaper-covered work surface. Give the board a generous coating of PVA adhesive and let it set for about ten minutes or, until the board takes up some of the excess water and the glue becomes tacky.

With the veneer assembly best-face-down on the work surface, flip the board over and set it glue-side-down squarely onto the veneer. It's best if there is a small, all-round overlap (FIG. 18-6).

Turn the sticky sandwich best-face-up and check that the design is fair and square with the board. Place the workpiece between the two clamping boards in the order of board, newspaper, plastic sheet, workpiece, plastic sheet, newspaper, and board. Make sure that the veneer is still perfectly aligned and top the arrange-

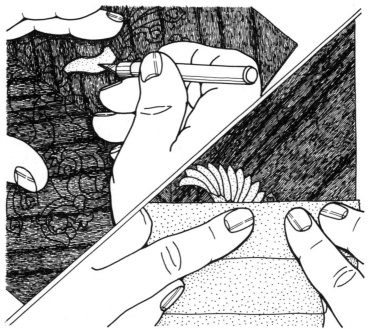

**18-5** Fit the cutout in the window and gently nudge it into place with the point of the scalpel blade (top). Tape the best face with single well-placed strips that run the length of the work (bottom).

**18-6** With the veneer assembly set best-face-down, set the board glue-side-down squarely onto the veneer—note the veneer should overlap the board slightly (top). Fit and fix the clock movement (bottom).

ment off with the bag of wet sand. Have a friend hold the veneer sandwich steady while you do this.

The glue should be dry in about 24 hours. At that time, remove the work-piece from between the clamping boards and make sure it is stuck down well. Set it best-face-down on the clean cutting mat and use the knife to trim off the veneer overlap. Remove all traces of masking tape and rub the work down with the graded sandpaper. Wipe away the dust and use the wax and a cotton cloth to burnish the face and edges to a good, smooth finish.

Support the workpiece with a muffled clamp and run the drill through the center of the clock—both the veneer and the board. Wipe the hole out with a scrap of sandpaper.

Finally, pass the clock spindle through the central hole, screw the clock movement in place on the back of the board, fit the hands, and the job is done.

## HINTS

When you are buying the matched veneers, make sure that they are consecutive sheets. Check the grain and, if necessary, number the sheets with chalk.

Double check the cutting and matching procedure before you put knife to wood. If you have doubts about the order of cutting, have a trial run with four sheets of stripy card.

Tweezers can be a help when handling very small pieces.

If you consider the knifeworked window design too intricate, you could stay with the diamond matching part of the project and simplify the motif to suit your own skill level.

If you don't much like the sand bag idea, look to other projects for clamping alternatives.

# Inspirational
# Pattern and
# Motif Directory

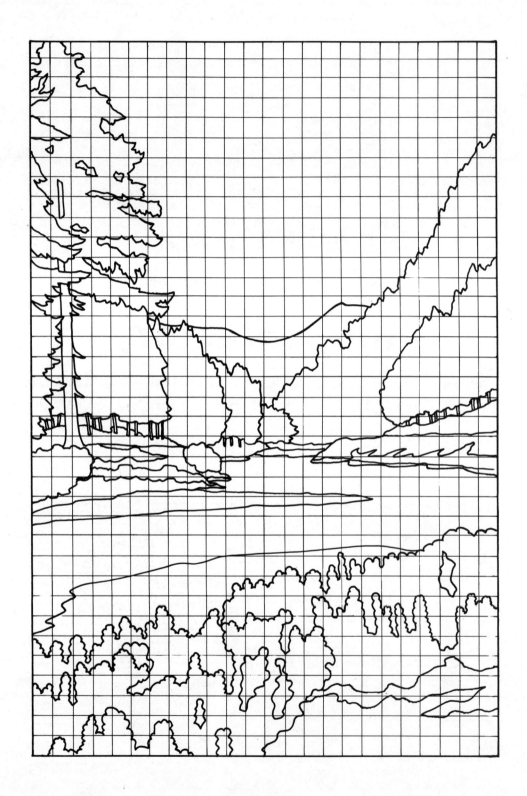

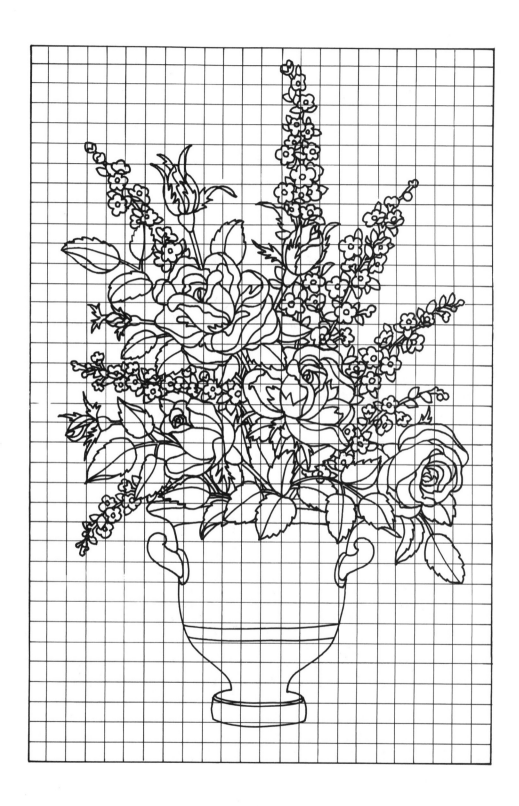

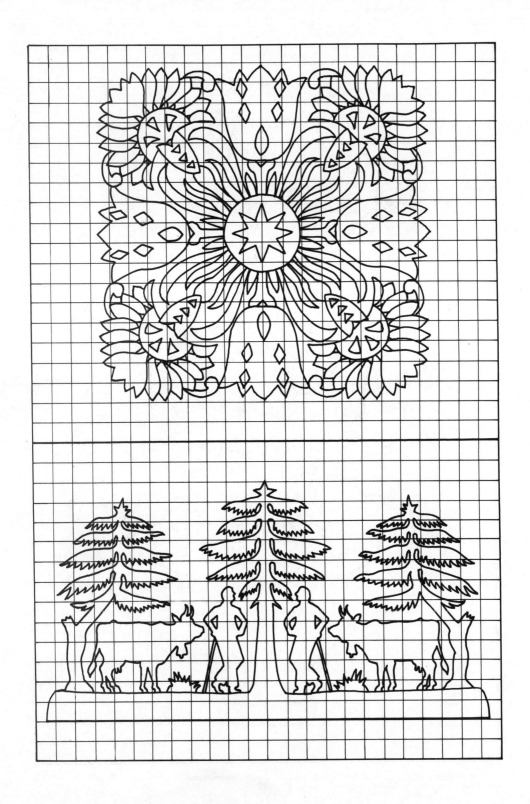

# Index